REFRAMING HOPE

REFRAMING HOPE

Vital Ministry in a New Generation

CAROL HOWARD MERRITT

THE
ALBAN
INSTITUTE
Herndon, Virginia
www.alban.org

The Alban Institute
2121 Cooperative Way, Suite 100
Herndon, VA 20171

Cover design by Spark Design.

Library of Congress Cataloging-in-Publication Data

Merritt, Carol Howard.
  Reframing hope : vital ministry in a new generation / Carol Howard Merritt.
    p. cm.
  Includes bibliographical references (p. 139).
  ISBN 978-1-56699-394-4
  1. Church work. 2. Hope--Religious aspects--Christianity. I. Title.
  BV4400.M447 2010
  253--dc22
                        2010025969

    10   11   12   13   14   VP   5   4   3   2   1

For Brian and Calla

contents

Foreword by Diana Butler Bass ix

Acknowledgments xi

Introduction: What Is the Substance of Our Hope? 1

Chapter 1: Redistributing Authority 9

Chapter 2: Re-forming Community 25

Chapter 3: Reexamining the Medium 47

Chapter 4: Retelling the Message 67

Chapter 5: Reinventing Activism 81

Chapter 6: Renewing Creation 93

Chapter 7: Retraditioning Spirituality 109

Conclusion: Hope in the Desert 129

Notes 139

Foreword

In his letter to the early Christian community at Corinth, St. Paul penned this memorable pastoral advice, "And now faith, hope, and love abide, these three; and the greatest of these is love."

Although these are beautiful and familiar words, I have always wondered if Paul was quite right. Over the years, I have heard hundreds of sermons based on this verse. Looking back, the vast majority have extolled the virtues of love and many have delved into the complexities of faith. Strangely, only a few explored the territory of hope. Like Paul, many Christians seem to prioritize the words: Love is surely the greatest and faith follows closely behind. But hope? Where and how does it fit in the Christian life, in pastoral ministry, in shaping community? Is hope more than a bronze medal finisher in the field of faith?

In *Reframing Hope*, Carol Howard Merritt offers an extended and elegant meditation—a practical sermon, really—on hope as a primary virtue of vital Christian community. Using both ancient and contemporary stories, she shows the connections between hope and love and between hope and faith, as she places hope front-and-center in the spiritual longings of young American adults. But hers is not a book about youth ministry, generational conflict, technology and faith, or planting an emergent church. Instead, *Reframing Hope* draws upon both Merritt's knowledge of postmodernism and her lived experience of being a young mainline pastor in the postmodern world. Thus, a hopeful story of the cultural changes that we all face unfolds in her narrative, a postmodern morality tale that offers insights about how the world and the church are becoming different everyday and how Christians—especially those who serve as pastors in faith communities—should *not* fear those shifts but can embrace and work with them.

Reframing Hope is written from the perspective of a "loyal radical," a postmodern pastor who leans toward "emergence Christianity" (a term borrowed from Phyllis Tickle, author of *The Great Emergence*), but one who is committed to a historic denomination (in Merritt's case, the Presbyterian Church USA) and its old buildings, handed-down polity, pathways of habit, and long historical memory. Loyal radicals hope to move into a vibrant future while retaining the wisdom of the past, balancing "wild freedom" with "the rooting and grounding of tradition." In these pages, Carol Howard Merritt articulates the passion of this "both-and." Through the power of storytelling, she explains and proves—yes, proves—that emergence and tradition must hold hands for Christianity to thrive in the twenty-first century. For Merritt, the both/and of emergence and tradition is more than a theory. She provides a GPS of the "re-"s: redistributing, re-forming, reexamining, retelling, reinventing, renewing, and retraditioning—the spiritual maneuvers that keep turning us toward a more vital life of Christian practice and deepened vibrancy in community.

Now, faith, hope, and love abide, these three; and, as Carol Howard Merritt reminds us, without hope, we might not ever truly understand or experience the other two.

Diana Butler Bass

Acknowledgments

I must admit, I'm rarely speechless—but the acknowledgments for this book have left me rather tongue-tied. There are so many people to thank, and when I imagine naming all the men and women who have touched this manuscript in one way or another, it's overwhelming. A network of bloggers, commenters, radio guests, chatroom participants, and Twitterers formed this work. Some of these individuals I know well, and others I've never met. All this has left me wondering: *How can I send thanks to a network?* The many conversations on TribalChurch.org and the relationships I've formed through Presbymergent, RevGalBlogPals, the Young Clergy Women Project, Transform, and Outlaw Preachers have helped me rethink communication and ministry in a new generation.

I am grateful for the group of clergy writers who gave me feedback as I envisioned *Reframing Hope,* especially Ruth Everhart, MaryAnn McKibben Dana, and Leslie Klingensmith. During the year, our dear friend and member of the group, Karen Blomberg, died. Throughout my writing, I ached as I missed her compassion and wisdom.

The *God Complex Radio* podcast crew inspired me, as I gained from their insight. I continue to learn from members of the crew, Landon Whitsitt, Mark Smith, and Heather Scott, as well as from all the conversation partners who have been guests, listeners, and participants. They helped me to put many of the ideas in this book into practice.

And I want to express my great appreciation to Bruce Reyes-Chow, not only for his fine work in co-hosting the show, but also because he and his wife, Robin Pugh, shared the Galax House in Montreat with me in a critical moment, allowing me a spot on the spacious porch where I was able to write the bulk of the manuscript.

Of course, I am always grateful to the people of my congregation, Western Presbyterian Church, who remind me that ministry is not just what happens within our four walls, and allow space for me to develop this avocation of writing and teaching to the larger church. Their passion and commitment to social justice inspirits me every day. And I want to thank John Wimberly, the head of staff, for his vision and support throughout the project.

I am blessed by the hard work of Alban Institute's publishing division, especially the insight of Richard Bass, the director of publishing, who recognized what I could accomplish even before I did. They have been patient and encouraging. I could not have written this book without my editor, Ulrike Guthrie, who has been prompt and tireless in her work on this manuscript. Uli not only shapes the ideas and words, but she also drives me to become a better writer. I also learned a great deal from the careful editing of Doug Davidson, who has an amazing ability to hold the larger vision of the work intact while giving attention to the small details. Doug asked crucial questions and persistently buoyed me until the manuscript's completion.

Finally, I could not have kept up a full-time job, a demanding travel schedule, and a daily writing discipline without the unbounded nurturing of my husband, Brian Merritt. Brian's encouragement has been a source of continued strength for me. And I'm always grateful for my daughter, Calla. Her laughter, love, and life incite me. It is for her that I write, in the hope that the world and the church will be a better place.

introduction

What Is the Substance of Our Hope?

As a church leader and writer, I often feel I'm in the midst of converging streams, trying to sort out the flowing torrents. The currents course so quickly that I find it hard to keep up with it all. Technological changes, generational dynamics, environmental instabilities, and philosophical understandings pulsate, making these realities difficult to frame. And yet, in this exciting and hope-filled time, I cannot resist trying to capture the movement.

During the last few decades, we've watched the attendance wane in many downtown mainline congregations as demographics shifted. White people moved out to the suburbs, leaving behind many predominately Caucasian congregations that did not know how to reach out to their new neighbors. Evangelical megachurches sprang up on the outskirts of towns, swallowing many of the mainline transplants. With bare exteriors and pleasant interiors reminiscent of shopping malls, these large churches filled with people attracted to charismatic pastors and catchy praise songs. For the last twenty years, eager leaders in mainline denominations have been looking to the robust megachurch movement to teach us how to reach out to our culture in a relevant way.

But that doesn't seem to be working any longer. As megachurch members age, worship as entertainment seems to be losing its luster.

Many evangelical pastors have become exhausted by trying to grow a church on steroids.[1] The children who were raised in megachurches are becoming irritated with the bigger-is-always-better attitude. Frustration with the megachurch model is growing, and attitudes toward evangelicalism in general have hit a new low.[2]

Now, as we reach the time when those of us in Generation X (born in 1961 to 1981) ought to be settling down in our religious habits, we find that many of us have not established any. The sons and daughters of those who abandoned the denominational structures that the mainline church built in the 1950s are now deriding the evangelical churches that grew up in wake of mainstream Protestant decline.

Not only have religious attitudes changed, but demographics are swirlas well. We can no longer trace an orderly pattern of white flight to the suburbs. Now we find rings of suburbs and exurbs, and the cultural makeup of our cities is changing yet again. Younger generations long for the diversity, arts, and earth-friendly transportation of urban centers. Highly skilled and educated men and women of every ethnicity are moving back into the very same urban areas many of their parents fled.[3]

As we catch glimpses of what is swirling, we may wonder where all this is taking us. And we know it is not just generational attitudes and demographics. We realize an important philosophical shift is also taking root, which leads us to ask: How do postmodernism and pragmatism change us and our congregations? How can the church adapt to flourish in this new context? What vital possibilities are arising in this exciting, surging time? How can we reframe our ministries—our faith, our hope, and our love—in the midst of these currents?

Why Should We Reframe?

Framing is a linguistic and psychological term. Frames are the basic mental structures that shape the way we understand the world. They are of limited scope, yet they have a systematic internal organization.[4] When we use linguistic frames, it is a bit like examining a picture. We know many things exist outside of what we see as we look at a photograph, just as we know there are realities beyond what our limited words can explain. A picture organizes the available information into something coherent that our minds can grasp and understand. In much the same way, framing allows us to focus on something in order to describe it—and as we do, we leave other things out of the boundaries. However, linguistic frames do not only limit our focus to what is present, they can also help us to understand our histories and imagine what our futures might be. They can point to the "now and the not yet," having a profound effect on how we think about and perceive the world.

My husband is a big fan of college football. When the team he roots for is not doing well, he will often talk about the current season as a "rebuilding year." I don't know much about football, so I always take his word for it—even when the year turns into a decade. The words create a hopeful frame that explains the discouragement of the present as well as provides excitement for the future.

There is something powerful in such framing, because it suggests that current frustrations are foundational for heartening things ahead. When our economy performs poorly, political leaders often put the dismal numbers into a particular frame by saying, "We are in the midst of an economic recovery." The term *recovery* acknowledges something is not right, but assures us it will be back on track soon.

Now, I have been a pastor in DC for the past five years. Is framing just a P.R. trick I've learned here? Have the spin doctors of the district had too much influence on me? No, I don't think so. Our words are important. The way we frame our situation has an impact on our current attitudes, our cognitive abilities, and our future behavior. As church leaders, how we frame our current situation is vitally significant. Indeed, it is part of the prophetic calling to name what is while at the same time imagining what can be.

As we talk about our particular church settings, we use frames. Often, these frames are narrow boundaries that focus on specific numbers. We look at membership gain or loss in a particular congregation or an individual denomination. We scan attendance records to see how many people showed up on a given Sunday or how our income compares to our budget. We consider the number of churches that open or close in a given year. Based on those numbers, many church leaders talk endlessly about how our congregations are in decline.

The numbers are important, but we can miss out on a great deal if we ignore the ways these particular numbers fit into a larger narrative. We can lose sight of our future possibilities. But if we can shift our focus, take into account where we have been, and imagine what God is calling us to be, our frames can open to a larger vision and a greater hope. We can begin to see the changing landscapes in our culture and understand the vital networks and essential streams flowing around us. We can name the possibilities.

The currents that flow in technology, organizing, communication, and spirituality in our larger culture deeply affect the way we minister and form community. Of course, the world is always changing, but the current economic and environmental realities have left us teetering on the brink of potential disaster.[5] Global climate change and the rise of the middle class have made our planet dangerously unstable. These dynamics have caused a new generation of Christians to consider the potency of new technologies, to evaluate the ways in which our notions of power, poverty, and the worldwide economy evolve, and to organize our spiritual communities in a different way.[6]

The church can make a couple of mistakes when dealing with rapid cultural change. The first is to ignore what is coming; the second is to take no heed of what has passed. Neither omission is healthy. Instead, our task is to look at existing things in a different context, with fresh tools, honoring the traditions and generations that brought us here, while imagining what we might become.

Barbara Brown Taylor noticed our penchant for ignoring the past when she taught Introduction to World Religions in a university.[7] She observed that her Christian students were able to talk about the history of religions other than their own. But when it came to Christianity, it was as if they'd skipped from the disciples mending the nets by the Sea of Galilee two thousand years ago straight to the streets of the United States: "They never thought about what happened during the centuries between Jesus' resurrection and their own professions of faith. In their minds, they fell in line behind the disciples, picking up the proclamation of the gospel where those simple fishermen left off."

This weakness in Taylor's students reflects our deficiency as church leaders. We often fail to appreciate our own histories and the streams of thought that have formed us, and we are not always able to recognize the liberating progressions within our tradition. Right now, there is a movement of Christians who hope to "begin at the beginning" and to create a Christianity that makes sense in a new generation. They long to set aside the church as it has been and look forward to forming a church for them. Particularly in some emerging church movements, we hear calls either to get back to the practices of the apostles and the first-century church, or to create the church anew, inventing it for the first time.

Should that be our goal? First of all, it's not possible. There is no way we can ignore the history that is a part of us. Even if we did not grow up in the church, when we step into one, that chronology pulses through our proclamations and our passions. Congregational independence, Reformed structure, Anglican tradition, Evangelical fervor—we cannot understand who we are unless we also understand from whence we've come. When we fail to recognize our history, we miss out on the great wisdom of previous generations. We delude ourselves into thinking we are the first ones to come up with "new" ideas while we disdain those who have come before us. When we ignore our traditions, we turn our backs on centuries of rich and wonderful thought. We shut out two thousand years of saints who have walked this same journey, praying fervently and teaching us how to commune with God. We ignore the life-giving liturgies that have inspired countless congregations. We close the books on libraries of theological engagement, veil the art that has uplifted our forebears, and silence the beautiful music that's been passed down to us.[8]

Not only that, but in order for our churches to heal and become whole, we also must acknowledge the dark valleys of our past—the religious wars and the bloody schisms that fill our history books. Men and women can become strange and dysfunctional when they cannot claim their own backgrounds, when they become too ashamed of the people they once were and repress those parts of their experience that feel too painful to face. Good therapy and support groups often work to reconcile an individual's past with his or her present so that person can grow into healing and wholeness. Likewise, in our congregations and our traditions, we become dysfunctional if we do not acknowledge the grief of former times.

As church leaders, one of the most important things we do is to try to figure out why there is mistrust in particular corners of our congregations. For instance, we may be aware that everyone involved in adult education has a difficult time trusting the pastor. What we may not know is that forty years ago the pastor had an affair with a Sunday school teacher. Somehow, that trauma stays within the system, even if people are unaware of it. Even though the indiscretion may have been hidden, and the individuals involved no longer present, the feelings of betrayal and the acute sense of heightened responsibility remain part of the congregational family.

When Christians ignore our histories, we cannot understand our present circumstances. Yet, when we begin a process of healthy disclosure, the wounds find the ministrations needed to begin the comforting and painful process of healing.[9] This holds true for individuals, for particular congregations, and for the church-at-large. Our histories, good and bad, are a part of us. We can begin to imagine vital church ministry in a new generation only by remembering that we have emerged from somewhere specific.

The act of reframing acknowledges the need for a new view at the same time as it recognizes the strength in our traditions. It allows us to look at the past with fresh eyes. Instead of slipping into value judgments—setting up dichotomies between the old and the new, the elder and the younger, the stable and the adaptable—reframing allows us to recognize possibilities simply because we are looking at our situation from a different perspective.

Just as we cannot erase our histories, we also cannot ignore the changes in our present and future. And so I write *Reframing Hope* understanding that the great shifts happening in Christianity in this day are part of a larger picture. We are not creating from nothing as we begin the vital ministry of the next generation. Instead, we are working through what we have, gathering up the best parts, acknowledging and healing from the worst, and reframing it in a new generation.

Why Hope?

I cannot remember a time when the church was the hub of society and life. I was born in the 1970s, part of Generation X. I never lived in a church-centered world. When older members of my congregation tell me about it, I can imagine what it might have been like, just as I can envision a time when people went to church three times a week. But I have never lived in that reality. I've always been in a culture where church was a place my friends visited on Christmas Eve—and now even that tradition is beginning to fade. I grew up in the midst of church news filled with clergy affairs, prostitution, and pedophilia. Throughout most of my ministry, I have worked in the shadow of these dark wounds of Christianity, laboring in a world in which the church is renowned for its sex scandals and conservative politics, a world in which people proclaim, "Religion poisons everything."[10]

This is the culture I know. And this, strangely, is the place I feel most comfortable. It is not that I am happy about our current circumstances but simply that I have not experienced anything else. When I introduce myself as a pastor at parties or neighborhood gatherings, I encounter little awe or respect. Instead, I am met with a ravenous curiosity, as if people did not even realize it was still possible to make that career choice.

Yet, as many mainline churches move farther and farther to the sidelines of our culture, as megachurches lose their entertainment value, and as denominational leaders look to the next generation, there is a great deal of hope waiting to be kindled. I find inspiration in our growing congregation at Western Presbyterian Church in Washington, DC, and in the fact that those who show up to worship here are drawn by a deep sense of community and search for God. I am encouraged by the larger landscape as well. The movement of young adults into urban centers and their ever-increasing reliance on local economies means the model that drove people to the megachurch is breaking down.[11] Urban congregations that did not fare well during the 1970s and 1980s are beginning to see new vitality.[12] The new pictures now coming into focus are shaped by changing demographics, shifting social concerns, and burning spiritual yearnings. As we look toward the future, we can see streams of living water bubbling.

When we consider the progressive political leanings of younger generations, we realize they long for spiritual communities that care deeply about social-justice issues—the same issues that our denominational congregations have been organizing around for hundreds of years. There is a deep spiritual yearning pervasive across generations, yet we know people will no longer settle for one-way preaching and entertaining services. They want meaningful worship, an empowered lay leadership, and a spirituality that leads to action. Again, people are longing for the very things that many denominational churches have been cultivating for decades.

Finally, the coming of age of the Millennial Generation (those born between 1982 and 2001) bodes well for our denominational congregations.[13] Not only is this generation much larger than those that preceded it, Millennials are also much more community focused and institutionally minded than the generations before them. Generational sociologists Neil Howe and William Strauss believe the influence of the rising generation will cause "every arena [to] become more mannerly, structured, and civic minded." With regard to religion in particular, Howe and Strauss suggest, "Millennials will favor friendly rituals and community building."[14]

If we begin to reframe the important work of our spiritual communities, taking care to understand the shifts occurring in our culture and to respond to them faithfully, then the years ahead can be extremely fruitful for us. If we realize and welcome the changes that will come, if we can be open to what new adaptations will bring to us, if we can begin to sense the Holy Spirit moving, then we will be able to sense vitality in a new generation.

We know from the words of Hebrews that "faith is the substance of things hoped for." And so this book is motivated by the question, what does the substance of hope look like *right now*, in the midst of these rapidly flowing currents? What is our vision of hope when it is framed in a new generation?

chapter 1

Redistributing Authority

On a trip to the Grand Canyon, our family decides to venture outside the national park and into the Painted Desert looking for art. We soon see a large, spray-painted sign on the horizon that promises "DINOSAUR TRACKS." It sounds too good to pass up.

After stepping from our air-conditioned car into the sweltering August air, we give a few dollars to a tour guide and follow him around the barren land as he points out ancient bones embedded in the red clay. We clutch our water bottles, sipping them frequently to get some relief from the oppressive heat and dry air. The young man has a bottle as well, but his is equipped with a squirting cap—and he uses the stream of clear liquid to precisely outline the bones and fill in the embedded claw prints.

There are, indeed, dinosaur tracks in the hardened clay. Not only that, but we also learn that the bits of red stone all around us, the same polished rock that graces so many pieces of locally crafted jewelry, is coral. Then our guide points out huge sections of the ground that are rippled and explains, "You can see that this area was once completely underwater."

Amazed, I crouch down, tracing the hard, wavy ground with my finger. On this day, in this dusty desert, I cannot imagine how it happened. I've read about these things in textbooks—how landscapes evolve, how plates shift, how animals adapt to new environments or become extinct. But I never thought I would stand in the desert and see clear evidence that it was once underwater.

When we get back into the car, my head is still spinning as I think about change. I wonder how long it took before anyone noticed that the plates of the earth were shifting. How long did it take for people to realize the masses of land were moving farther away from each other, changing the nature of what sort of creatures could survive in their new habitat? How long did it take before we noticed the slow movement, before the chaos of it all began to make some sense, before we could understand the nature of patterns that seemed so random?

Habitats change, physical landscapes shift, and humans evolve. Our very bones adapt to different circumstances and environments. Our intellectual, philosophical, and religious thought adapts and transforms in each generation. Just as the plates of the earth shift, just as our spines straighten, our own understandings of God and the church are shaped and transformed by our context. Right now in our culture, things are rumbling and moving beneath our feet. Everything is shifting.

I stand in the middle of it, feeling the rumbling. Spiritual traditions, generational wisdom, theological engagement, international compassion, and environmental concern are all moving. I observe the busy swirl as the Spirit moves in and among it all. Working closely with "loyal radicals" of the Presbyterian Church (USA), I notice old traditions being reclaimed by a creative and innovative generation, hope being carried off and reframed, and new vitality coming to the church through it all.

I see evidence of such change and innovation regularly in my work as a pastor. I often find myself snooping around old books, reading about another time and setting, gleaning from the wisdom of the past, borrowing resources from other traditions, and reframing practice and thought in a new generation. Of course, that's nothing new; church leaders have always done a bit of that. But now our libraries are not just physical but digital as well.

The Internet has made rare texts available at my fingertips. No longer am I forced to drive for miles to cull through theological collections. I can scroll through entire libraries while sitting on my couch sipping a cup of hot tea on a Thursday afternoon. I can sort through current academic ideas, up-to-date research, and ancient texts. If I want to delve in further, I can use the Web to buy books, journals, and papers that were once available only at the most specialized bookstores. Such easy accessibility, coupled with the fluidity of American religion,[1] allows me to borrow from other traditions, sorting through the wisdom of the ages and reframing it for practice today.

But I'm not only looking at the flat text. New technologies are allowing individuals to spark one another's imaginations and share resources. I find myself in the midst of constellations of thought that formed without carving out particular locations or even specific times for people to converse. A spirit of collaboration and open-source ideas has grown up in our culture so we can easily share resources and information with one another.[2] More and more, these exciting conversations include voices from people outside of mainstream publishing, and the publishers themselves are looking to blogs for new writing talent and to bloggers to extend the conversation about current books. Ideas that once might have caused small sparks inside our academic institutions can now catch fire and spread beyond the traditional ivory tower, as more professors begin blogging and we have wider and easier access to academic papers. This shift affects every segment of our society—and especially the church.

Knowledge (and therefore, power) is moving from the centralized institutions—our seminary bookstores, theological libraries, and academic institutions—to the margins, creating a new network of pastors, church leaders, and other public thinkers. The diffusion of authority is sweeping like a wind over our landscape. In the shifts that are taking place, we feel the breath of the Holy Spirit, blowing through conversations, relationships, and connections.

As a pastor and the mother of an eight-year-old daughter, I'm aware that just ten years ago, I'd never have been able to accomplish the amount of research I can today. Now, many streams of thought feed me all the time. While my daughter works on her homework or plays outside, I can engage in theological conversations, write, and think. I regularly converse with people all over the world about what happens in their churches.

This explosion of thought, innovation, and ideas points to the fact that in vital spiritual communities we are reframing our faith and hope. In our religious landscapes, as information and organizing abilities spread to the margins, authority shifts. With the philosophical movement of postmodernism and the technological developments of the Internet, new communities spring up, and something exciting unfolds.

We can see it happening in many different places—through the emerging church of the postevangelical movement as well as the "loyal radicals" of the denominational church, in the formation of new monastic communities and the revitalization of sacred traditions in liturgical congregations.[3] God works through both our passionate love of the church and our anger toward it. The progressions are not just occurring among certain age groups or denominations but across the chronological spectrum and throughout our traditions. In every corner of the church, the tectonic plates are shifting.

The change that surrounds us today will be much easier to describe retrospectively a few decades from now. But I will try to articulate what I am seeing now, to frame the cultural, technological, and church movements from my perspective as a pastor working now in the midst of vital denominational congregations deeply involved in social justice matters.

Although I will be writing about issues as large and complex as the environment and globalism, I will paint the picture from my limited viewpoint: as a pastor, who goes to work each day, ministering in a new generation; as a writer, who pounds out regular blog posts and articles, connecting with varying perspectives; and as a speaker, who travels across the country and the world engaging in conversations with various groups and denominations. I will give you a glimpse of what I see, from my standpoint.

Cultural Movements

To set the landscape of our current movements, to see the larger reasons why this transfer of power to the edges has occurred, we turn our attention to what is transpiring, philosophically, in our postmodern context. I visited an exhibit on modernism at the Corcoran Art Gallery a couple of years ago, and I was stunned at the contrast between the perspective between that time and our own.[4] What optimism people possessed about human ingenuity and all that we could do! One display featured a film of a highway system, in which the narrator said, without a hint of irony, that with highways, there would be no more stopping on the roadways.

Pulsing through all the exhibits was unbridled confidence. Underlying each painting, urban development plan, or kitchen appliance was the abiding notion that technology would be the answer to everything, that our own inventions would solve every domestic headache and increase our productivity. Each corner had an exuberant, commercial-like proclamation that the right conveniences and gadgets would lead us to a better life. With our ingenuity, we could find our way out of any crisis and our creativity would usher us into a day of freedom and leisure.

Much of it happened just as we imagined. Technology gave us the dishwasher, the clothes dryer, the birth control pill, and the choice for women to enter the workforce. Our innovation and resources allowed us to move from an agrarian culture to an industrialized culture. With our humming mixers and beeping microwave ovens, women have a new freedom from domestic responsibility and freedom for education and financial security. Women can settle into corners of our society where we could never have found a place before—even the pulpits of our churches.

The overall spirit of modern society was an unbounded optimism that things were getting better; they were always improving. Markets would always grow, and things will forever increase in size and scope. There would always be progress, and our children would be better off than we were. This is the culture in which most of our Christian education buildings were built and our systems of church governance were honed. We constructed steeples in the midst of this optimism.

Yet the reality of postmodernism also began to seep more and more into our popular culture, and our narratives as a people changed. The Civil Rights movement and the women's movement unfold, speaking out against the many pervasive social injustices. The Vietnam War protests, the assassinations of the 1960s, Watergate, and a whole string of other events prompt citizens to question those in authority, particularly the government. Mistrust grows and breeds. Somehow, all of a sudden, in place of the certainty of a better future ahead, apprehension begins to taint everything.

Our nation's faith in people in powerful positions took a tremendous hit during the 1960s. By the time I was born in the seventies, this distrust in the promise of power and technology were a loud and clear part of our national narrative. We no longer see cars flowing in perfect sync. Those utopian highways look more like parking lots during the hours when we most need them to flow. We are finally figuring out that the exhaust fumes belching out of tailpipes are changing our climate in drastic ways. Now, when we witness the construction of bigger highways, we're savvy enough to realize they may lead not to faster transportation but to yet more cars, more pollution, and a quicker demise of our planet.[5]

Technology once gave us such hope. Now we look beyond our windshield wipers and realize we are entangled in traffic patterns we cannot negotiate or resolve.

However, the most profound shift that has taken place as we've moved from the modern to the postmodern world is not one that we perceive outside of our car; instead, it is something sinking in in the drivers, something we hold within us, something that looms in our minds and heart, just barely breaking through our conscious understanding, but always there.

Children today grow up with the knowledge that while technology has greatly improved some aspects of their lives, it has also given people the ability to utterly and completely wipe out humanity. From my earliest years, I have known that our weapons have grown immense, and this possibility caused me—and my entire generation—to tremble with fear. With that seed germinating within us, with that knowledge of good and evil, we have come to understand the dark side of our creativity. We no longer have the luxury of being blindly optimistic. With realization comes responsibility. No matter who we are, we know we have to assume power. We recognized we cannot afford to trust mindlessly. We have learned to be vigilant in questioning authority. And as we grow up, we learn to challenge, doubt, reason, and test almost everything.

The effect of this shift in responsibility has led us to organize differently. In a new generation, when we make decisions, learn, create, and build, we instinctively construct a network to do it. We're not comfortable taking orders without question and not content having the weight of power in one person, so we have learned to imagine, dream, and dispute together. Almost everything we do has taken on a communal quality, and our most popular technologies fuel a social sense of the collective.

Those spiritual communities that welcome these shifts of power will be the ones that will thrive in the years to come. Vital churches will not be those that rely on their denominational brands to draw people through their doors but those that have something creative and compelling to say about what is going on outside those doors. Growing churches will be centered on sharing conversations among those journeying a path together rather than the one-way preaching of an unquestioned authority. Effective church leaders will not look at the networking occurring in a new generation as superficial, rude, narcissistic, or indiscreet but will begin to understand the deeper realities of what's occurring in this larger conversation.

In our current culture, two forces are pulling us in opposite directions. On the one hand, there is a movement to more centralized power. And, in reaction, there is an increased empowerment of the edges. Let's take some time to examine each of these trends. First, we will take a look at the move toward conglomeration.

Conglomeration: The Bigger-Is-Always-Better Culture

Many of us often feel a sense of powerlessness because so many of the resources we need to live come from a concentrated source with which we have very little connection. Our news, entertainment, clothing, food, and basic goods originate from a handful of mainstream corporations, who do all they can to ensure they can reach as many consumers as possible. People are constantly encouraged to want more, which leaves us with gut-level frustration.[6]

We work under the assumption that continued growth is essential. For a business to be successful, for an economy to be vital, for a church to be healthy, it must be growing—rapidly. Yet, this corporate conglomeration, with its unwavering pursuit of continued growth, has resulted in a loss of community and connection. We no longer borrow money from a local bank staffed by friends who have an intimate knowledge of our family situation. Instead our mortgages are sliced up and sold to numerous lending companies until the act of lending is far removed, and the identity of the borrower as well as the mutual responsibility that was once so necessary in such large transactions has become lost.

This loss of connection is not just apparent in the large things but in small things as well. I know that the head of lettuce I buy at the supermarket takes a journey of a thousand miles, wasting petroleum and polluting the air before it reaches my dinner plate.[7] We are often forced to buy our goods from big-box stores, dragging ourselves through miles of aisles, despairing of ever finding an employee who might answer a simple question. Adding to the frustration, we know the money we spend will not benefit our own hometowns.[8] Even our once proudly independent and quirky coffeehouses have been taken over by giant corporations. Now the commercialized coffeehouse replicas can be found on highway exits, situated between McDonalds and the truck stop.

We no longer know how our shirts are being made, who's making them, how much those workers are being paid, how old they are, or how long their working hours are. We gave up a whole lot of our own influence on how our vegetables should be grown or how many hormones ought to be injected into our poultry. Children do not know where food comes from, and they are often stunned to learn that the chicken on their plates is the same thing as the chicken on Old MacDonald's farm (which itself has become more or less a distant memory).

We feel hopeless in our political climate as well. Angry and frustrated by the wars, lies, and torture perpetrated in our country's name, we seem to be powerless. No matter how massive the protests are, no matter how passionate we are about ending violence, stopping genocide, or feeding starving people, we have a dispiriting sense that a few people with a lot more money are making the important—but not always good—decisions on behalf of all of us.

What does all this have to do with the local church? How does this conglomeration of power in our culture, this shift that can be felt in our commerce, affect our ministries? Well, just as our downtown churches grew up in the optimism of the modern era, megachurches are one of the defining religious trends of this bigger-is-always-better culture. Founded on the outskirts of town, the megachurches overshadowed our neighborhood churches by their sheer scale. Suddenly, there was an expectation within the pastorate of leading a church with a membership in the thousands. Programs became so much bigger and ostensibly better in these huge churches that people would flock to them from miles away. People were no longer looking for the big steeple of the downtown congregation but the big parking lot in suburbia.[9] Members no longer sought a pastor with whom they could share a family meal and confide in during times of crisis, but a charismatic star who could preach an exciting and entertaining sermon that would invigorate them and get them through the week.

When I first became pastor of a small church in rural southern Louisiana, the Fruit of the Loom factory in the town had just closed down. Since that had been the town's main source of employment, there had been a population exodus. The residents left there were mostly retired, unemployed, or situated well below the national poverty level. A large segment of the population could not read. I felt called to that place, even though I knew full well that the demographic data did not support the likelihood of immediate and massive growth for the local Presbyterian congregation.

Yet, when I spoke about my new vocation, there was an expectation that if I did my job well, the church would increase in size—and not just incrementally. People seemed to expect this small rural congregation would become some sort of megachurch within just a few years. People would tell me what kind of programs had made their church grow, or about their charismatic pastor who created a booming congregation in the middle of nowhere, and members would drive for miles just to be a part of it.

I would try to explain that I was not walking into that sort of situation. I was going to a small, downtown church that used to be the center of the community's communication and entertainment, but it was no longer the focus of community life there. Things had changed in the little town. But the expectation persisted that under the right sort of leadership, with just the right pastor, the congregation would become something that it was not. We would meet in pastors' groups, where the men (I was always the only woman) would compare the sizes of their respective congregations, and then the guy with the biggest church would impart his wisdom to the rest of us.

The pressure was external, but I have to admit that it became internal as well. The assumption that success equaled quick and massive growth loomed over me. Even though the church did expand at a healthy pace, I never felt I was doing quite enough. The well-intentioned members would often assess the situation: "Things are going great, pastor." And then they would add, with urgency, "Now how are we going to get *more* folks in these pews?"

The model for ministry had changed since the time when a downtown church attracted a couple of hundred members. We were living in a bigger-is-better time. The new expectation was that a congregation wasn't truly vital unless it was attracting thousands. That was the assumption, and yet, it clearly was not the ministry we were doing best in Abbeville. We were growing a small, intergenerational community.

Everywhere I looked, from conferences to books to denominational gatherings, I saw little support for churches like mine. Educational materials were way out of our price range, and we could not touch the technology "they" said we needed. There were no resources and few models for solid church ministry in the small church. Those few congregations teeming with thousands of members were celebrated, but there seemed to be no room for the rest of us.

In this milieu, pastors and churches become understandably tired. Church growth is no longer about a steady 10 percent increase but about how to attract thousands in less than ten years. Churches are no longer "planted"—now they are "launched." We're encouraged to study these superchurches and emulate their programs and services. In the process, the size of the congregation has become what matters, instead of the quality of the community, or the spiritual vitality, or the formation of faith. Evangelism is no longer a sacrificial service devoted to spreading the good news and serving as a beacon of hope for individuals and our neighborhood. Instead it has turned into a self-serving exercise to get "those people" into our building so that we can construct even bigger buildings and larger programs. As a result, people outside the church view the new generation of Christians as uncaring and see the church's evangelism efforts as manipulative.[10]

The net effect is that church leaders and congregations alike are left feeling as if we are not enough, and as if we will never be enough.[11] Then, depleted and defeated, we pastors forget our calling: to take care of the handful of people there every Sunday who are a part of our spiritual communities, to challenge them to see the deep hunger and needs of the world around them, and to figure out how we can become the hands and feet of Jesus. We forget that people go to church for the same reason they've always gone to church—not because it is the biggest and most entertaining place in town, but because they have in their core a spiritual longing to be fed.

From our produce to our political power to our pulpits, we decided bigger is better. We opted for less personal contact. We began to lose sight of what is good for our communities and began to focus on the individual. However, the bigger-is-always-better attitude left us empty, anxious, and depressed.[12]

Meanwhile . . . Along the Edges

Amid this frustrating, hopeless conglomeration of commerce, right in the middle of our bigger-is-always-better attitude, and even as the megachurch has become the model of what church ought to be, something else is happening. There is a slow but perceptible movement to the edges. The fringes of our society and our spiritual lives are looking better and better. A new generation is reframing hope as we begin to see the beauty and richness of caring communities.

Just as the conglomeration has happened in every area of our culture, the movement to the edges can likewise be detected in many spheres of society, including our entertainment, information, news, and politics.[13] As we move toward music and books that do not need hard media, companies do not have to rely on stocked inventory and limited warehouse space. Therefore, they can provide more options. With more choices, people are beginning to look for music from smaller bands or publications that may never grace the *New York Times'* bestseller list.

Farmers markets are gaining popularity as we realize just how much damage big agribusiness is doing to our earth and how much petroleum we consume by shipping produce from all over the world to our refrigerators. More and more people are digging up patches of their lawns so they can create gardens. Realizing their children will actually eat their vegetables if they have a hand in growing them, busy parents have bought hoes and now aspire to growing the perfect tomato.

As the stock market crashes, volatility shakes our economic foundations. We are beginning to pay dearly for the skyrocketing housing costs that outpaced our salaries long ago. We are starting to understand that rampant growth can wreak havoc on a society, especially when it is fueled by ever-increasing debt.[14]

We are beginning to realize smaller might really be better—or, at least, that there ought to be limits to growth. We've realized what we've been missing in our big box stores on our seemingly endless walks under the fluorescent lights—meeting anyone who might be able to talk to us and help us. More and more, we're turning off our televisions and finding value in homegrown entertainment. And we are finding great spiritual vitality in our neighborhood churches, the ones with smaller parking lots and communities of people who really know and care for one another.[15]

In this innovative generation, people are using emerging technologies to communicate with one another, to let their voices be heard, and to express their frustration with the conglomerating markets and entertainment. Alongside cynicism, frustration, and powerlessness has grown an ability to call out in small ways. Unfortunately, this option is not equally available to everyone; there is a digital divide that tends to make the gap between the haves and the have-nots even wider. Yet, we cannot ignore that there has been a shift when we review our homegrown entertainment, questioning of information, empowerment in the political system, and conversation in our religious communities. Let's take a moment to consider each of these areas a bit more closely.

ENTERTAINMENT

More than a decade ago, MTV launched its first reality television show: *The Real World*. The concept was simple enough: Take a group of (sort of) regular people, put them in a house together, and film whatever happens. Since then, we have seen countless "reality" shows, these documentaries of common life. Likewise we stage huge, televised talent shows like *American Idol*, where the audience members vote to determine who wins.

At the heart of this entertainment trend is the celebration of the noncelebrity. The ordinary becomes entertaining. And a new generation has taken this to amazing heights. We went from television networks producing reality shows to people creating such shows themselves. YouTube has become a way for people to take their living room entertainment and broadcast it to the world—and people are watching. Blogs have become a platform for people to self-publish their own insights, rants, and reviews. Social networking sites like FaceBook allow us to connect with friends and strangers from around the world. And it is all very entertaining—so much so that television is losing a whole generation of younger viewers.[16]

Of course, our culture's fascination with the celebrity has not disappeared, but we seem most interested in the ways in which the celebrities are just like us. We like to read about the glamorous singer who ventured onto the red carpet in a terrible dress, or onto the beach with embarrassing cellulite, or even into the rehab center with a heartbreaking addiction. We become fascinated with celebrities who remind us that they have fabulous wealth, stunning talent, and terribly unglamorous humanity.

News Media

The power of media is shifting thanks to a new generation that rarely picks up the morning paper. We no longer gather around the five o'clock evening news to learn what's going on in our world. Rather, we rely on Internet news sources and media we can talk back to, with comments. While Dan Rather may once have been the unquestionable authority, the *Washington Post* now hosts online chats with its journalists. They have realized they can no longer present themselves as the unquestioned experts if they want to engage a new generation. It is no longer enough to have a degree from the right school or years of experience; journalists need to be open to dialogue and discussion. In fact, it is just as much through handling these conversations that they gain their expertise. I write a blog for the *Huffington Post*, and I'm fascinated by the publishing changes this innovative news source represents. While they may not have the fact-checkers and editors of traditional newspapers, with so many viewers commenting on each post, factual errors quickly come to light. We use Twitter to share news, information, and observations with those who follow us, and over time, these form an ongoing discussion. Through posting articles on Facebook, we can rapidly gather a discussion on pertinent news as well.

In the same vein, the trend of fake news and news parodies has grown from a short weekly segment on *Saturday Night Live* to a nightly hour of Jon Stewart and Stephen Colbert. The online and print publication *The Onion* has gained huge popularity with its faux headlines. Each of these sources encourages us to pick apart our cultural assumptions, question our authorities, and laugh and play in the midst of fearful situations.

Politics

Few have understood these cultural shifts better than President Barack Obama. No matter what our personal politics might be or how we evaluate his presidency, I would be remiss if I didn't mention Obama's 2008 presidential campaign in this context.

President Obama's commitment to community and grassroots organizing, as well as his understanding of young progressive Christians, made his campaign incredibly savvy about how a new generation communicates. At the very beginning, his campaign hired a designer from Facebook to set up social networking on his website. Since I don't watch much television, I never saw any televised ads for the Obama campaign. But I repeatedly saw a moving YouTube video that featured Obama's soaring words accompanied by the vocals of will.i.am from the Black-Eyed Peas. The video was sent to me through e-mails; it was posted on blogs I read regularly; I saw it through my social networks.

I found these videos much more powerful and compelling than traditional televised political ads because they were introduced to me by trusted friends rather than by corporate America. Obama understood better than any major political figure before him that his campaign would get credibility not only from influential men and women supporting him but also from word-of-mouth, as one friend told another. In addition, many of Barack Obama's most captivating visual posters were not designed by a Manhattan advertising agency; instead, they came from a well-known graffiti artist named Shepard Fairey. The designs literally came from the streets. Obama understood that in a new generation, reliable information does not radiate from a central power; rather it moves underground, through networks, streets, relationships, and friends.

During the campaign, Obama's message of "Yes, we can" was more than just a logo or a hip-hop song. It was his way of doing business, as he empowered a new generation to resist the cynicism that corporate and political power can foster. It allowed ordinary people to dream, to imagine how they could change the world. And it acknowledged the important shift in power from "he" to "we." And that transference generated great hope.

RELIGIOUS COMMUNITIES

Nadia Bolz-Weber is a Lutheran pastor and author who has written a book about Christian commercialism. Reflecting on her work in a recent interview, she said, "I used to get upset about the fact that millions of people love Joel Osteen, but then I remembered that millions of people love Hot Pockets, and that made me feel better."[17] While it's easy for us to become frustrated with the religious conglomeration that grows up alongside and so closely mirrors our consumer culture, we can also celebrate the fact that shifts are occurring toward the edges of our Christian culture as well.

We see the movement in minor ways. The Internet has made the cost of reaching a worldwide audience quite small. I have appreciated the effects of this diffusion of power in my own writing. At first I sat hunched over my computer, laboriously writing magazine articles and sending them out to various publications, only to receive rejection letters. Then I began a blog, and as I posted those same articles on a website, I began to gain a substantial readership. Magazines and newspapers I'd never even submitted to because I assumed they were far out of my reach began linking to my blog and turning to it as a resource. Before long magazines and book-publishing companies were contacting me, and I quickly realized that my writing did not solely rely on the traditional channels within the publishing industry.

I remembered that my mother, with the same writerly intentions, began a small newspaper when she was about my age. The difference was that she had to buy the presses, paper, and postage. She relied heavily on volunteers to put the physical product together. It was an ambitious and expensive task. Now, after the initial investment in a computer and the cost of ongoing Internet service, my mother and I have both learned to write blog posts and press "publish." As long as I keep the conversation interesting and post regularly, people keep coming back.

As a result, I have become a part of a larger network of bloggers (most of them pastors) who read and exchange ideas constantly. We dream of changing the world and write funny stories about what the people in our churches said as they shook our hands after worship on Sunday morning. We share mundane frustrations about Sunday school supply rooms that are never left clean and try to figure out what to do about poverty and the environment.

Those are small examples, but we can also see the huge and dramatic effects of technology, even within religious movements. In the fall of 2007, Buddhist monks in Burma began to withhold the alms bowls from military families as an act of protest. Instantly, the world saw what was happening, despite the country's closed government, because of cameras on cell phones. The pictures were taken and sent all over the world by e-mail.[18] Suddenly, people across the globe saw the brutal images of the peaceful orange robes being stained with blood. Cellular capabilities were quickly shut down, but the information was already out. The world was aware and could express its horror because regular people with mobile phones in hand gained momentary power over a forceful regime. As the prayers of U.S. Christians joined the cries of those young Buddhist monks suffering half a world away, we knew something had changed. Even in that most authoritarian of regimes, a bit of power had shifted so that briefly the oppressed had a voice.

In tragedy, protest, celebration, and Christian formation, we grapple with the optimistic advances and enduring suffering to which our technology has testified. We realize how speech, influence, and even our religious convictions have shifted a bit to the edges. Now, in this exciting moment in history, when so much is in transition, we are forming new religious communities and finding vitality in older congregations, and we are reframing hope. It is in this time that we religious leaders who inhabit the outskirts and the edges must look anew at the ways in which we gather.

chapter 2

Re-forming Community

"How do we reach out to a younger demographic?" This is the key question many churches and denominations are asking—and it's not only out of a concern for institutional preservation. Instead, church groups genuinely care about young men and women, and want to live out their mission in ways that reach out to a new generation.

It was with this goal in mind that a church-based organization sought to begin a mentoring program a few years ago that would reach out to seminarians and young pastors just starting out in the parish. I was one of those young pastors. The organization intended to select a few Really Big Names to mentor us, assuming young pastors would be drawn to get involved so that they could spend some time with a Big Name guru.

When the staff person from the organization began listing names of possible mentors, one young participant interrupted and mentioned the name of someone who was about her age. She was seeking a mentor who was a pastor and writer, but also a networker—a blogger skilled at creating online community and facilitating discussions.

The irritated organizer said, "No. Not him. We need an *expert*. Really Big Names."

The mentoring program never got off the ground, and I am not surprised. In the meetings, there was a palpable disconnect between the organizers and the would-be participants. The organizers thought young pastors would be drawn in by one-on-one connections with respected intellects, while the participants wanted people who looked like them, understood what they were going through, and could have a cup of coffee or an online chat with them. Respected names, doctorates, or seminary posts would have been a bonus, but for the most part, the younger pastors were not drawn to the famous preachers or scholars but to people who could create connections and nurture community. They looked to people actively engaged with social media, bloggers, and colleagues. More importantly, they saw mentoring and discernment as part of a wider conversation, something that happens in a group rather than one-on-one.

For me, the incident marks a generational reframing of mentoring styles, leadership, and learning. A collegial model has replaced the expert model. The young pastors of an earlier era might have felt honored to have even a few moments with a recognized expert who was normally available to only a select few. They might welcome an expert's coming from the mountain and dispensing a bit of wisdom before leaving us to return home mesmerized by his or her lofty degrees, positions, and accomplishments.

Things are different now. Currently, we expect mutuality and interaction. We look for a leader and mentor to be a hub; to be connected to many others; to be accessible, authentic, and human. We are reframing leadership and learning to value most those leaders who help build community.

In the following pages, we explore the substance of our hope by asking some vital questions about the nature of leadership and community. Why are communities so important in this particular generation? What does vital spiritual community look like? What kind of church leadership truly builds such community? And these lead us to deeper questions: If we move to more fluid and open organizations, are our denominational structures completely outmoded? In what ways are these structures still important?

The Importance of Communities in a New Generation

Though I am part of the postmodern generation, my answers to these questions are largely a product of my work with a broad spectrum of generations. When leading workshops on developing intergenerational congregations, I often ask, "What sort of political, religious, economic, and social movements defined your generation? What events did your generation go through that made you who you are?"

In different parts of the country and around the world, the themes that emerge in these workshops are often very similar. A fascinating chronology emerges through a cacophony of voices. Through this peopled history, we can hear how our thoughts and attitudes have formed, and we learn how the cultural and societal changes in each generation affect our church movements.

Older men and women tell about living through the Great Depression and how frugality shaped everything they did. People learned to open up their homes for family members and tenants. Even though many years have passed, those who lived through the Great Depression distinctly recall the trauma of scarcity—and, therefore, continue to rinse out plastic bags, reuse coffee grounds, and stretch one meal for a week of leftovers.

Next the stories about World War II unfold, as men and women remember what it was like to live on rationed food, milk, and gas. Because so many men were fighting, these narratives often include stories of what women of that period were doing. The feminist movement bloomed during the war effort, as white women dropped off the kids with a grandmother or aunt, rolled up their sleeves, and went to work in factories—joining the many African-American women who were already working. After the war was over, the spirit of sacrifice and hard work did not end, but men and women redirected that energy and the nation's resources to build many of this country's institutions. Of course, our mainline congregations were central in this growth, as many of them were formed in the midst of postwar optimism and the construction of our country. People of this generation are known as "Builders" for good reason.[1] They constructed the infrastructure of our country and provided the bricks and mortar for many of our institutions. Many Christian education buildings were erected through the proceeds of bake sales and quilt auctions.[2]

At the same time, a sense of entitlement sometimes characterized the wealthiest families of this generation. Educational institutions made admission decisions based on legacy, and success in one's professional life often had to do with whether one belonged to certain social clubs.

This ensured the dominance of certain families and particularly but-tressed white, Anglo-Saxon, Protestant culture. The members of our mainline churches were often the educated elite—the ones who ran the banks, businesses, and law offices.[3] From what I hear echoing through the crowds gathered at these workshops, authority felt quite different then. People rarely questioned parents or teachers, there was a deference toward pastors, men and women trusted the government.

Then, the scene quickly changes as people relate stories of huddling under school desks as small children. The terrified boys and girls were enacting mandatory drills, using the tiny tables in a meager attempt to shield themselves from an imagined nuclear attack. If they were in hallways, the children learned to back up against the concrete walls for safety. In other exercises, boys and girls ran home as rapidly as they could so their mothers could time their arrival. It is no wonder that these children began questioning what was happening around them as they grew up. A culture of distrust was piqued during the Vietnam War, the Watergate scandal, and Richard Nixon's resignation. Young people encouraged one another to "never trust anyone over thirty."

The Civil Rights movement called into question many long-standing assumptions of the white, Anglo-Saxon, Protestant culture. New voices arose, offering new visions of greater possibilities for our country. Even when fire hoses and angry dogs threatened, men and women continued to march for dignity and respectful treatment of African-Americans. Women demanded equal money for equal work. The country seemed on the verge of a new progressive era, until things took a tragic turn. The assassinations of John F. Kennedy and Martin Luther King Jr. dashed our dreams and shook our nation's confidence. One of the many casualties in this dark time was trust in our public institutions. With a growing belief that our government and institutions could no longer be depended upon, the foundations of all we'd built began to crack, and a period of autonomy and individualism arose.

The Immigration Act of 1965 abolished national-origin quotas and opened our borders to a rich variety of people from non-European countries. In our academies, a subtle shift occurred, with entry into colleges becoming based more on special exams as opposed to legacies. While inequities remained, Ivy League schools were increasingly open to bright men and women of every ethnicity. So our population—including the elite—became much more culturally diverse.[4]

My voice joins the narrative at about this time. When I was in elementary school in the late 1970s, even children knew that school drills and a mere writing table would not shield us from the enormity of nuclear destruction. Instead, I grew up in the Ronald Reagan era, with friends who schemed how they could become millionaires before the age of thirty. We talked about the "Arms Race" as if it were a new Olympic sport. The Cold War threat of Russia haunted all our social studies lessons and gave our country the excuse to produce more and more nuclear weapons.

As we built powerful and destructive bombs, we dismantled our modern age. Our technology, we realized, not only had the potential to make our lives more convenient and entertaining, it also had the force to *obliterate the world*. A 1983 TV movie, *The Day After*, seemed to encapsulate this fear through its detailed depiction of what would happen if there were a nuclear attack. Walking the campus of our junior high school the day after that movie aired, everyone seemed to tremble with the horrifying possibilities.

We men and women of Generation X, born between 1961 and 1981, grew up as "postmodern." We are often characterized as cynical and questioning; but as products of this new reality, we have also developed a new sense of responsibility.[5] While our parents may have learned to challenge authority through experience, we were taught from the start to question the words of people in power. Many of us grew up as latchkey kids in broken homes, letting ourselves in the front door after school, turning on the television, and waiting for mom or dad to get home from work. We were taught to believe complete independence is the key to a healthy life. Rebellion was understood as a natural part of development and was even encouraged as a stage that would help us to separate from our parents and allow us to become more independent.

With the numerous school shootings and the events of September 11, violence has never seemed only something far away, in some distant land. It was always a possibility—not just in the next big city, but even in the next classroom. Through all these experiences, a new generation inherited a greater culpability for destruction and responsibility for one another. They could no longer trust institutions in the way that their grandparents may have; there was too much at stake.

The Yearning for Community

Theologically speaking, it was as if a fall had occurred. With total eradication possible, our naivete had to die—and in its place a new responsibility grew up, making us into a wary and suspicious people. In that fallen reality, we realized technology was a seed of both good and evil. We had new accountability as citizens and could not trust our leaders blindly. We developed a survival practice of questioning everything. Our lives—in fact, our planet's very existence—depended on it.

Each time I listen in these intergenerational gatherings, as our shared story arises throughout this fifty- to sixty-year time span, I recognize a slow shift from modernism to postmodernism. The modern mindset was characterized by an optimistic belief that history was moving in an upward sweep, that technology was a tool for greater good, and that the institutions and structures of authority that surrounded us were worthy of our trust. Postmodernity encompasses the realization that we humans can and are ruining our planet and obliterating our means of existence—often because of the same technology that once gave us such hope. It is within that reality that postmoderns look for and work for progress. It is with that concern that we have questioned institutions.

And yet, as a country, we realize complete autonomy and independence is not the cure for our cynicism toward authority. Young adults found we could not make it on our own. Because of the increase in college tuitions, housing costs, and medical care that came along with stagnant salaries, many young adults are buried under a mountain of debt, leaving us dependent on banks and parents to get by. Furthermore, we've discovered that all that inculcated autonomy, individualism, and consumption did not make us happy. We recognize that in pursuing economic stability and independence, we've often neglected to build up our families, friendships, and communal lives, and we've become weary, depressed, and anxious.[6]

With the economic situation increasingly dire, we recognize our need for the support of a community. We are beginning to understand ourselves as persons with gathered "friends," and we make sense of the world through networks and tribes. Our technology reflects our yearning, and through amazing innovations, we gather communities and stay connected by virtually sharing status updates and vacation photos with a hundred of our closest friends across the world and throughout the day and night. We publish our thoughts, engaging in constant conversation with both people we know well and others whom we've never met. We look for mentors who will join the dialogue, and we value men and women who do not mind being engaged in concerned questioning.

Community within Religious Movements

What has been happening in our churches during this shift? What does this small sweep of history look like in our congregations? Just as men and women have been formed by the events in their cultures, their churches have also been shaped by culture. In the fifties and early sixties, our mainline denominations grew up in the postwar boom, with civic-minded pride, and the dominance of white, male, Protestant culture.

The attitudes toward institutions and the changing role of women are particularly interesting aspects of the shift in the decades that follow. In the late sixties and seventies, many people in our culture began to develop a distrust of institutions, and the denominational church began to wane. When a minister entered a store wearing his clergy collar in the fifties, he got a discount. When the same minister entered the store in his collar in the seventies, he got dirty looks.

While our culture was striving for autonomy and putting a high value on the individual, denominational churches were characterized as social clubs, filled with people who showed up to show off the fact that their children had nicer clothes than anyone else. But as the country clubs waned and the people on the golf courses got older, many of our churches (especially the ones that mirrored country-club behavior) lost membership as well. At the same time, a vibrant evangelical culture began to sweep across our nation, with a strong emphasis on an individual, personal relationship with Jesus Christ. Denominational congregants were often seen as people who simply did not take their individual devotion seriously.

In the late eighties, some evangelical congregations became quick to adapt cultural fads. They abandoned the heavy hymnals, projected words on screens, added contemporary Christian music, and encouraged the megachurch model. A Christian consumer culture grew up that reflected what was happening in our malls: we began to think of a healthy congregation as a place where thousands of people meet. Many congregations wisely focused on the "seeker," those who were burnt out on the denominational congregations or who had given up on church altogether. They no longer expected the people who walked in their doors to be comfortable in the particular culture of a denomination or church in general. Understanding the changing religious attitudes of their time, many evangelicals did not expect the Boomers to attend their parents' congregation. They realized the need to create something new. In the early nineties, Willow Creek became an example for many congregations, with their stadium seating, drama performances, and relevant messages. The era of the institutional church was over. People were not interested in making sure that their grandmother's congregation survived; they needed something for themselves, something that would nourish them on an individual level.

Faith was personal rather than communal. "God has no grandchildren," I was often told in my megachurch youth group. "This is a decision that *you* make yourself." Sacraments like communion were hardly ever celebrated in the churches I attended as my faith was being formed. Programs catered to every particular group in the church. Autonomy and a smorgasbord of options at church were in.

The autonomy that we nurtured in our religious life began to seep over into our political landscape as many evangelicals were drawn to Republican policies that valued the individual's ability to pull oneself up by one's own bootstraps, and allowed enormous holes to appear in the societal safety net for people who needed it. We American evangelicals did well at loving God and loving ourselves but our individualistic spirituality did not always translate into loving our neighbors when it came to policy matters.

Meanwhile, as all of this growth and vitality was occurring in the evangelical church, something very interesting was happening in our denominations. Though it was a time marked by cynicism and distrust of the institution, though we suffered considerable decline in membership with many Boomers leaving their parents' congregations to do things differently, it was also an incredibly exciting time, especially when we think back at what the shift looked like for women.

When World War II was over and the troops came home, the white women who had briefly entered the workforce resumed their domestic duties. However, new technologies were making it easier for women to work outside of the home. The dishwasher, washing machine, and clothes dryer allowed women to complete household chores more quickly, yet we still did not have an economy, childcare system, or societal understanding that supported a flourishing professional female workforce. More women began attending college and entering the educational system or the secretarial pool, but when a woman married or became pregnant, she was expected to go back home and stay there. So what were women doing with all that energy, intelligence, and imagination once their children went to school? They found a place where their gifts could flourish. As sure as the bricks and mortar, women began to build the church, with all their talents and volunteer hours.

Often the congregation was the center of a woman's life, and so it followed that her spouse and children were expected to attend services every Sunday. Religious education flourished thanks to women who taught Sunday school and led Bible studies. Women's groups grew up within our denominations, complete with gifted officers, abundant budgets, and full schedules. These circles became powerful influences on denominational structures as they built alternative bases of influence outside of the traditional religious hierarchies.

But in the late sixties and early seventies, when more women began to keep office hours outside of the home, they had less time to create and maintain volunteer opportunities in their congregations. In our churches, our robust volunteer workforce dwindled along with the women's groups.

Yet, in academia, our theological worlds began to open up as a result of our questioning power and attributing more importance to community. A broad and beautiful spectrum of women and men of various ethnicities began to challenge our small focus on white European male thought. Our seminaries filled with the voices of the liberation movements as we began to understand the incredible diversity of faith stories.

Women began to permeate our denominational seminaries, first as students and then as professors. Women began to fill our pulpits. We gained a new chorus of voices, voices that questioned how stories were interpreted, voices that explained how they saw the words and world differently than the accustomed perspective. They breathed the life of the Holy Spirit into the text and community. No wonder that people who were born at this exciting moment of exploding thought were particularly affected.

The Turn of the Century

Many of the young evangelicals who grew up in the metal folding chairs of these huge congregations began to reject the uncomfortable political alliances their parents and pastors had made.[7] They were wary of evangelistic techniques that seemed to focus only the number of people who had made decisions to accept Jesus into their hearts, rather than caring about their whole complicated, questioning lives. When many young Christians realized economic autonomy might be out of their reach, they began to challenge capitalism and the ideals that were championed by the Republican Party. Disturbed by a religious culture that looked disparagingly on women who worked, many became increasingly frustrated with churches that focused on reproductive choice and homosexuality as the key moral problems in the United States. Now, some estimate that one thousand people are leaving the evangelical church every day.[8]

Which brings us to our current religious milieu. We retain the cynicism that remains wary of institutions *yet* we are weary from radical individualism. Many of us became tired of bearing our own burdens in congregations where we were not allowed to question or wrestle with our faith. A new generation is longing for authentic community, a place that nurtures our spiritual lives and develops deep concern for one another. We look for groups that understand the need for both individual responsibility *and* communal action. We seek religious communities where our salvation is not dependent on a litmus test of belief or adherence to a particular code of behavior. We seek communities of faith that will hold us, communities within which we submerge ourselves into a river of sacred traditions centuries long.

The leaders we seek are not the remote experts who dominate institutions or the charismatic rock stars who entertain and encourage us in our personal relationships with Jesus. Instead, we look to people who are willing to build community, form tribes, and walk alongside us. We look to leaders who share the path in our journeys, who make mistakes, who have time for conversation.

Along with this shift from isolation to belonging, we can also realize the incredible amount of innovation that presently takes place. William Strauss and Neil Howe describe those born between 1961 and 1981 (Generation X) as "the greatest entrepreneurial generation in U.S. history."[9] In speaking about their preferred occupations, three out of five people say they want to be their own boss. Strauss and Howe also note that this age group includes the largest share of immigrants, and our "high-tech savvy and marketplace resilience have helped America prosper in the era of globalization." It is a generation known for taking things apart and putting them back together in a completely different way—whether that involves how we listen to music, read a newspaper, publish a book, or talk on the phone.

We are doing exactly that in our churches. In this time, we are taking apart what we have, examining it from different perspectives, wondering what it will look like in a particular neighborhood, and questioning whether existing leadership styles make sense. We are starting our own churches and developing new kinds of spiritual communities. We are experimenting with different models of sustaining pastors in smaller churches. We are reaching back to historic models, imagining what those practices would look like in a new context, and asking important questions: Will one pastor be leading a number of communities? Will pastors become bivocational and depend on another source of income? Will churches become bi-vocational and learn to make money by running another business?

Of course, such questions and innovations are not confined to one age group. But this generational research is a good indication of what is starting to happen in our religious culture right now. With such tremendous fecundity in our present pastoral leadership, I cannot wait to see what becomes of it.

In the midst of this yearning, we see new movements rising and converging all around us—new monasticism, postevangelical emergents, the multicultural church, the outlaw preachers, and those Phyllis

Tickle calls the "hyphen-mergents" (Presbymergents, Anglimergents, [D]mergents, Methomergents, etc.) who mingle the sensitivities of the emergent movement with their own long-standing denominational traditions. I tend to refer to these men and women as *loyal radicals,* because Tickle's terminology suggests that those us in this group will eventually have to choose between our denominational structures or the emergent church.[10] Unless we are kicked out of our denominations, most of us have no intention of leaving—yet we fully realize we are a part of a shift in ecclesial thinking. We feel comfortable with the tension of working in a denomination, even with the reality that we live in a postdenominational culture.

Although there are many similarities between loyal radicals and those who identify as *emergent,* there are also a number of important differentiations. I will highlight three. First, loyal radicals are distinctive because of our strong ties to our histories. We appreciate the theological richness of our social justice, liberationist, and feminist traditions. We celebrate the vital spiritual disciplines that form us. We have a hope for a vibrant church that makes sense in a new generation, we are open to innovation and creativity, yet we also appreciate the wisdom in some structure.

Another important distinction between the two groups concerns their origins. The postevangelical emergent movement grew out of a meeting organized by Doug Pagitt, who was working at the Leadership Network. The meeting gathered a group of highly gifted men in hopes of identifying who would be the next leading voice of evangelicalism— the Bill Hybels or Rick Warrens of Generation X. That meeting led to a number of growing friendships among some of the participants. Many of these men found themselves wrestling with postmodern thought and deep theological issues they did not feel free to talk about in their congregations or with other colleagues. Several emergent leaders met at this gathering, and Doug subsequently formed relationships with Tony Jones and Brian McLaren. McLaren, Pagitt, and Jones write passionately, their thought is provocative, and their friendships have been generative. And though they are not the official leaders of the emergent church, their spirits and intelligence flow through the movement, and they claim its creative origins. They create hubs of discussion and events where relationships form and deepen.[11]

I've come to appreciate much of what McLaren, Pagitt, and Jones have to say. But at the time when people first start calling me an "emerging leader," I'd never read any of their writings, and to this day I've never met McLaren or Jones. I appreciate their work, but my own stream of thought does not originate with them. While my evangelical upbringing informs me, it is my progressive mainline tradition that feeds my theological hunger. And I'm not alone. Many loyal radicals are growing up alongside the postevangelical emergent movement. Although there may be some overlap in thought, many of the young church planters, pastors, writers, and leaders who are doing innovative work in our churches today do not trace their origins to the postevangelical movement. In fact, some of these leaders are very reluctant to have their work associated with a movement that has been vehemently antidenominational and too closely tied to evangelicalism.

The third way in which loyal radicals are distinct from postevangelical emergents is in our attitudes toward women, ethnic minorities, and lesbians, gays, bisexual, and transgender persons. Although most postevangelical emergents are open to the inclusion of women and some are open to LGBT persons, there are others in the movement who do not think that women or LGBT persons should be leaders. Post-evangelical emergents see leadership as organic, so they expect men and women to step up into positions, believing the door is open to anyone who would like to walk through it. But it's clear that straight white men find their way through that open door most frequently. In contrast, for loyal radicals, racial diversity and the leadership of women and LGBT persons is imperative. We realize that *especially* in our religious cultures, men are often socialized to take leadership positions, while women and LGBTs are subtly and blatantly discriminated against. Women and LGBTs might resist naturally stepping into positions of leadership, and so we feel a responsibility to actively engage and empower those who might be resistant to leadership. We are more adamant about full inclusion of all people; we confess and take responsibility when it does not happen. Even though we often fall short (especially in ethnic diversity), we demand representation, rather than being passive about inclusion.

Even as many denominational churches continue to mourn their membership decline, a new generation of Christians is longing for the very practices of inclusion, diversity, and questioning that many mainline churches have been cultivating for these last few decades. Though some postevangelical leaders see our institutional structures as fortresses of power that work to keep people out, I am thankful for the structures, not because of any power they might have, but because of the empowerment that they offer.

Importance of Denominational Structures

I learned the distinction between power and empowerment during college. I applied for a job teaching children at a local art museum. Although I had no formal art training, I hoped I could get it on the strength of my portfolio. The museum director looked at my work, told me it was lovely, then handed the giant folder back to me and sent me on my way. "We have so many people floating around our community with art degrees," she said. "We really cannot hire someone with no training."

A couple of weeks later, the phone rang. It was the director telling me they had, in turn, hired several professional artists, and each had left the job. The children were too difficult, too rambunctious. So the museum decided to give me a shot since I had a lot of experience in teaching children.

I went to my class and was surprised at what I found. The room was in utter chaos, supplies were scattered about, older children were bullying younger ones, and no one was heeding my instructions.

The next day, after a long conversation with a friend who teaches elementary school, I came more prepared. I had a list of five guidelines the class was going to abide by. They were simple instructions that most classrooms have. With that small suggestion of structure, we had some order, and children could hear directions, ask questions, and work without being bullied. As a result, creativity flourished. A sense of security allowed the children to concentrate, and in the safety of the environment, the students knew they would not be teased for their creations and that their work would be protected from destruction. Within the protection of the environment, their imaginations sparked and inspiration could flow freely.

While teaching these classes, I left the nondenominational church I'd been attending and joined the Presbyterian church. I found parallels between what was happening in the museum class and in my denominational setting.

I was a young woman, an introvert, with a strong call into ministry. As I looked around for an opportunity to serve in a nondenominational congregation, it seemed the church allowed only a certain sort of person to be in charge. Although that voice of vocation—the one beckoning me into church ministry—was growing louder, I did not have any external affirmation. When I explained to church leaders that I wanted to go into the ministry, they scheduled a day when I could help the secretary in the church office. I knew I looked nothing like the type of person who always seemed to become pastors in our congregation: tall, good-looking, extroverted men.

Then I joined a Presbyterian church. It was through the structure of the denominational church that I was able to gain the education and support to live into my calling. Even though I knew its people were fallible and its structures imperfect, I felt a sense of security in the democratic organization. It was a system that encouraged women and men to have equal voice, that supported me as I pursued my call, and that allowed me to obtain a seminary education. Through that system, I was able to find the empowerment I needed to minister in an academic setting that allowed me to fully question.

The organic leadership model, where pastors are raised up through the community without the shackles of a denomination, did not work for me—and I daresay that model probably fails to work for countless other women, as well as some historically disadvantaged minorities. Just as children in a classroom needed parameters in order to be able to create beautiful pieces of art, I needed the structure of training and the voices of support that came from my community so that I could begin to hear God's calling and live out that creativity.

Although many emergent church leaders point to the denominational church as an unredeemable bureaucratic structure that stifles innovation and is inseparably bound to modernism,[12] I have a different experience. I found denominational congregations to be less hierarchical because they encourage the leadership of women more and have a longevity that allows the community to thrive long after the pastor is gone. In comparison, when a church rises up around a charismatic leader, the congregation tends to dissolve when that leader leaves.[13] There is comfort in knowing a congregation is going to survive long after the current pastor is gone. Even if a denominational church has to go a couple of years without a pastor, one has the assurance it will do fine because denominational structures support the development of strong lay leadership.

This does not mean the denominational church will be without challenges in the years to come. We will have to shed our great expectations that our church will be the center of life and society. We will need to realize that many of our congregations were formed in a white, Anglo-Saxon, Protestant culture that rarely questioned authority, and our culture has moved far away from that makeup and those norms. We will need to embrace the ways in which this new generation forms community. But we also have many gifts for a new generation. Congregations that have opened themselves up, allowing postevangelical refugees to heal and encouraging innovation and friendships, are seeing glimpses of hope.

What does this mean practically? How is community lived out in our faithful life together? What do vital spiritual communities look like right now? We can see communal ministry flourishing in a variety of settings, but I will discuss three: new communities, nesting communities, and traditional communities.

New Communities

It is evening as I enter the new church and see a group of people gathering together in an old repainted garage. In the worship space, I notice the beautiful table, set up in the middle of a semicircle of chairs. On the table there are the grapes, bread, and wine of the Eucharist, as well as a large pot of soup, and the scent whets our appetite for the things that are to come. Hanging from the ceiling above the table is a large piece of paper with a common liturgy written out by hand.

The service opens with a call to worship and a song. As the music begins, no one uses a hymnal, and the melodies are chants or choruses that we easily sing. Our simple voices rise up in prayer.

The service moves into moments of confession, where people have plenty of time to be silent and to name their sins out loud. The worship leader does not rely on participants reading details from a written order of worship; rather, she explains what we are doing and why we are doing it, and the descriptions allow us to become more comfortable in each liturgical act. Scripture is read, and I recognize it as a part of the week's lectionary texts. After the words are spoken, we are silent for a few moments, digesting the verses, until the leader invites us to share parts of the story that resonated with our own lives. One by one, different people share a single word or a story in response to the lectionary passage. Then the preacher begins her homily, weaving the reflections of those gathered into her own meditation.

In response, the community gathers around the table, for communion by intinction, as each person breaks off a piece of bread and dips it into the wine. We are then encouraged to pray at a series of stations set up in different corners of a room. In one corner is a place where you can light a candle and pray with an icon; in another is a table set up with paint where you are invited to create in images or words. Other stations include a basket where people give money, a place where worshipers can write down or draw their prayers, and a font where we can touch the water and remember our baptisms.

The evening ends back at the table with a shared meal, as we take the communion bread and eat it with some soup. Throughout the service, there is a sense of movement and openness. There is a hope that people will not only receive and listen to the word of God, but that people will be able to taste, touch, smell, and hear their prayers in the community.

In this gathering, people bring the best aspects of their traditions. The Presbyterians put their iconoclast history on hold and learn to pray with icons. We loosen our expectations of the order of worship that so often binds our time together and become open to the free-flowing worship of a charismatic gathering. Others jettison the evangelical custom of a long, teaching sermon in favor of a more interactive conversation. We pray the liturgies of the Episcopal church. Through the meditative silence, worshipers borrow the contemplative practices of Quakers.

This is not a service that most members of the congregation I serve in Washington, DC, would slip into easily, nor would I want them to. We have a tradition and style of worship that is comforting and meaningful to our congregation. Yet I cannot help but realize that there is a depth of community here, a sense of sharing in the burdens, heartaches, and celebrations in these gatherings that we sometimes miss in our larger gatherings.

New communities face many challenges. The style of worship works best with a smaller group and appeals to a younger demographic that may not be in a financial position to give enough income to support a full-time pastor.[14] These communities often have adaptable worship spaces and need minimal money for programming, but they typically find after a short time that having the support of dedicated pastoral leaders is crucial to their existence. Many of the wonderful, creative ministers leading these communities labor under considerable stress because of finances. When new communities start within a particular denomination, the governing structures may become frustrated with the rate of growth or annoyed by the fluid retraditioning they see in the worship.[15]

Could our denominations begin to come alongside these ground-breaking pastors and support them so they can keep creating worship services that make sense in their own communities? Could our governing bodies allow them to try, to fail, and make space for their successes? Could we realize that these church leaders are our innovators, working in liturgical laboratories right now, setting the trajectory, the mission, and the culture of our congregations for the years to come?

Nesting Communities

While many new worshiping communities are founded independently, others arise when established congregations begin nesting new communities. When we hear about such arrangements, many of us think of the 1980s model in which many evangelical and mainline congregations began holding a second "contemporary" worship service at a different time. These churches were able to keep the younger members of their congregations happy by changing the music style in one service. (The sermon was usually the same in both services.) But what's happening today is more than just changing the songs and rearranging the furniture.

Nesting communities are a liturgical response to a deeper cultural change. In many ways, they are similar to a model used in our denominations for decades in which a new congregation ministering to a particular immigrant population forms in partnership with an existing congregation. The two congregations may have different services, sharing their sanctuary space on Sunday evenings or Saturday nights.

When existing congregations find themselves unable to reach out effectively to a new generation, they may need to begin looking for other church communities they can take under their wing and begin to nurture, allowing them to minister to an unreached group in their community. Of course, many congregations find it painful to admit they are unable to reach out in a different culture, and they certainly do not want to give their space up to a new community that's competing for the same young, vibrant demographic they've been trying to reach. However, there is a crop of innovative, young ministers who want to start new communities. What if our established churches began to support them with a space? This is also an incredible opportunity for creative ministry to begin taking root in our churches, and we need to do whatever we can to encourage it.

As we look at the swelling generation in their twenties, we realize they are even bigger than the Baby Boomers. If our denominations can become innovative and imagine how we can reach them, this could be a vital time of growth for us.

Traditional Communities

But in addition to these innovative new communities, something else is springing up in our midst: a longing for the ancient traditions we have preserved in many of our congregations. And while new communities are taking root in some places, we are also seeing exciting growth among the kinds of churches in which I serve and am fed: intergenerational, liturgical churches, with a strong emphasis on both social justice and spiritual traditions.

Many of our urban congregations that suffered decline during the suburban exodus are having a steady revival. Many young, post-evangelicals have begun attending because they long to be a part of a tradition that flows strong and is not dependent on the pastor. People who grew up as atheists, with parents who mocked religion as shallow and antiintellectual, are beginning to explore what's happening inside of our walls, and they are finding a faith that takes deep questions and important intellectual streams seriously. Feminists who have spent the last twenty years hearing religious leaders blame them for all of the ills of society are being fed in places where women and men have equal power. Young activists who were nominally Christian growing up are being drawn by the shared passion and hope that we can change the world.

The members who enter our congregation, Western Presbyterian Church, are politically progressive. They are concerned with ending wars, fighting poverty, caring for creation, and supporting same-gender relationships. Many people in our congregation have "come upstairs" to worship after years of regularly feeding the homeless in the basement of our church.

The preaching is central on Sunday mornings. Although the preaching is a monologue during the service, we encourage discussion of the sermons throughout the week, through e-mails, blog comments, and podcast feedback. Most people in our church, even those who consider themselves to be postmodern, would not feel comfortable in a new community. Yet they do connect in our service, with its progressive message and traditional worship.

New communities and traditional worship are two vital streams, both pulsing with life. They bubble up, supporting new longings in our generation. Often they are supporting one another and working together.

Both emerging church and denominational leaders can be quite strident in their ideals and commitments, often adopting an either-or approach that finds little value in the other. Some emerging church leaders view denominations and their congregations as modernist structures that stifle creativity and innovation. They feel the only way to communicate the gospel in ways that will make sense to a new generation is by forming new communities. At the same time, some denominational leaders shrug off new and emerging communities as a ridiculous fad led by a few angry young men. Often, when I speak about these shifts with mainline church members, they greet me with knowing nods, occasional eye-rolls, and the same comments: "We've seen all of this before—the house churches, the coffeehouses, the intentional communities. All this already happened in the sixties."

I do not doubt there are similarities. But I hope we will not be quick to dismiss the spiritual longings of a new generation with a "been there, done that" shrug. Young Christians are often the ones who set the spiritual trajectory for future decades, and this is a time when vital new movements need to be encouraged and supported.

There are also people who are longing for both-and. We appreciate the strong social justice work, the vigorous theology, and the traditions of the progressive mainline churches, and we also welcome the creative, Spirit-filled dialogue that emerges with innovative communities. We know vital ministry in new generations is happening in new church plants, and we will encourage new communities as much as we can. But we realize that not everyone is in a position to start a new congregation. We realize that many new churches that spring up in a our generation are reaching new people who may never have attended church, and they are using a much more cost-effective model for church starts than our denominations have used in recent years.

As our churches reach out in a new generation, as we acknowledge everything that has changed since the flourishing years of our congregations, we understand the cultural differences of a postmodern generation who thinks communally. Frustrated by institutions and weary from individualism, a new generation thinks in terms of creative, breathing, open networks.

We are reframing leadership and community, moving from competition to sharing, from the pyramid to the network, from creeds to conversations. We can welcome the innovation of a new generation by encouraging and supporting new communities and by welcoming them into our traditional congregations. When the life span of an individual church has come to an end, we can plant new congregations and see what happens when these seeds take root in such a vital new day.

chapter 3

Reexamining the Medium

I'M ONLY HERE BECAUSE MY SERVER IS DOWN. —T-shirt on a guy meeting with friends at a coffeehouse

I didn't realize Nancy wanted me to come by until I started getting general complaints about my lack of pastoral calls. During the first year of my ministry, I had pulled out the church rolls, started with A, and began making my way down the list, checking off each person as I visited. I was making several pastoral calls each week, yet I still heard grumbling. I remember staring in frustration at the log I'd compiled detailing the various people I had seen and the hours I had spent in their living rooms, feeling that I would never satisfy the congregation no matter how many visits I made.

It took me awhile to learn that the congregation's perception of my pastoral calls had less to do with the quantity of hours I spent in members' homes and more with getting to particular homes. When a bike has a squeaky wheel, you don't need to spend all afternoon spreading oil on the handlebars and seat—just wherever the noise is coming from.

"Who most needs a visit?" I finally asked one of the wise church matriarchs, a former librarian who still makes it her business to keep abreast of all information.

"Nancy needs a visit," she responded. "Her husband died a year ago and, you know, it's just so hard."

I head off to Nancy's house at the first opportunity. Rolling past the main streets of the tiny Cajun town and into the small section just north of the rice mill, I admire the thick oak trees and dripping Spanish moss. The summer heat has definitely set in, but the sprawling wisteria doesn't seem to notice.

I often go under the speed limit in this town. At first it was just about avoiding a ticket. My speed declined drastically when I saw the list of minor traffic offenses that appeared in the *Abbeville Meridional* each week. I knew I didn't want "The Rev. Carol Howard Merritt" to be on that list. But eventually the slow pace of everything around me began to lull me into a different rhythm. I realized that I had no reason to rush.

After arriving at Nancy's place and peeling my legs off of the scorching vinyl car seat, I wait for several minutes at the front door. Nancy cracks it open just wide enough to see who rang, but she remains poised to close it in case of danger.

"Good afternoon—" I hesitate right before uttering her first name, relieved that the *n* sound never escaped my lips. The custom in this part of country, due to my young age and gender, is to call her "Miss Nancy"—which is confusing, because male pastors my age don't call women "Miss" anything. I'm not sure how important the title is to Nancy, and I want to be respectful, but I'm also not willing to accept any inequality with the men, so I leave it with a smile.

Nancy opens the cracked door and receives me into her spotless living room. As my eyes adjust to the cool darkness, I'm amazed at the lack of clutter or dust. I've been told that the women in our church used to wear white gloves when gathering for morning Bible studies in one another's homes. Then, when the hostess stepped out of the room, one of the guests would run her fingers over the doorposts to check on her domestic housekeeping skills. I never wear gloves on my pastoral visits, but the good housekeeping habits of my parishioners persist. Every living room I sit in is amazingly clean.

After I offer a few initial compliments on her garden, Nancy disappears into the kitchen for several minutes. When she emerges, she is carrying a tray of late afternoon coffee. I spring up from the couch and ask if I can help with the service, but she declines. So I sit back down and wait for her to hand me a fine china demitasse cup with a miniature silver spoon.

This is my favorite part of these visits. As I notice the polished silver and the china so delicate I can almost see the living room light through it, I'm aware that these items have made it down from the high shelf and into my hands. Holding the dainty spoon with two fingers, I'm reminded of tea parties I arranged for my dolls as a child, except this is no toy set: These are the special-occasion dishes.

I try not to wince with my first surprising sip of the thick chicory coffee. This stuff would knock the hardiest Starbucks barista off her feet. But I've grown accustomed to the strong coffee served here—at least enough that I don't think I'll be up *all* night after drinking it.

I spend the entire afternoon with Nancy. It takes that long to sip the half-cup and to hear her stories. She mostly tells me of her beloved husband. She tells me a bit about his life as a lawyer and armchair theologian, but she mostly talks about his death.

She knew there was something wrong, but her husband wouldn't go to the doctor. Looking back, she's not sure if it would have helped, anyway. She tells of how he got up from bed in the middle of the night to use the restroom, and when he got back under the covers, he gave his wife a groggy kiss, told her he loved her, and reminded her where the lawyer's phone number was kept.

She rolled over, wondering if he was still half asleep, since it was strange for him to be talking about the Rolodex at 3:00 AM. When she woke the next morning, she was surprised to find him still in bed beside her. He was an early riser who always sneaked out of the covers before she did. When she gently shook him, he was no longer breathing.

I've heard the details countless times. Before I understood this sacred ritual of widowhood, I had the urge to say, "Oh, yes, I know about this. You told me this story before." Of course, I could never do it. There is no way to interrupt this sort of narrative; it is much too precious. Even though I know each detail of those stunning days so intimately that I could fill in her next word whenever Nancy pauses, I would never attempt to do so. She needs to form the phrases and finish the sentences. I simply sit for the next couple of hours, nodding my head and holding each word of her story as carefully as I do the fragile demitasse.[1]

I learned incarnational ministry there in Abbeville, Louisiana. I understood that I needed to be there, in the flesh. And on hot afternoons, I would sit for hours, listening to beautiful accents. I'd set aside my to-do list for one more day, because ministry in such a setting is not about how many things I could accomplish each day. It's about seeing my parishioner's face. It is about making sure that her sad eyes still have a bit of a spark in them and that she can still care for herself and her home. It is about Nancy knowing she can call on me if she falls, and about answering her children's wary questions when they call. I cannot do any of these things unless I am here, in the flesh, taking careful consideration of her situation.

That visit with Nancy was less than ten years ago, but my pastoral visits have changed drastically. I no longer sit in spotless living rooms, meeting face-to-face with my parishioners. Here in Washington DC, I work primarily with young families, young professionals, and college students. In fact, I recall the look of anxiety I got early in my pastorate here when I asked a busy mother if I could stop by for a visit at her home.

"Why?" she asked after her shock wore off.

I picked up on the cue and quickly suggested, "Or we could meet for coffee. How about lunch? I could go to a place near your work. It's just that I . . . I wanted to get to know you a little better. That's all."

I knew what she was thinking, because I've been in her shoes. A young mother who's working a full-time job while also caring for her small children, keeping up with the mountainous laundry, and trying to cook relatively healthy meals isn't spending much time sitting in her spotless drawing room, polishing silver and waiting for the pastor to call. Schedules, availability, and expectations are all quite different today. Nowadays if the pastor asks to visit, the parishioner figures that she must be in trouble—or that a large building campaign has just begun. Church leaders need to find other ways to stay connected.

In this chapter, we will look at those other forms of connection, considering how interfacing communication (communication between computers) occurs, the hopeful possibilities it opens up, and the dangers that could result.

From Face-to-Face to Interface

My pastoral care professor in seminary instructed us to meet each member in his or her home during our first year at a new church. It was sound advice at the time. But there has been a change, a deep and abiding shift my good professor could not foresee.

In a rapidly evolving culture, people are no longer home during office hours. The church can no longer expect moms to host Bible studies in their living rooms at 10:00 AM every Tuesday. And if a pastor visits unannounced, he or she will probably be greeted on the front steps, and will remain there, standing, for the quick duration of the call. In just a few short years, pastoral visits have changed dramatically, along with all of our communication.

I remember when it started. Seventeen years ago, my husband was working at Sam's Club, in the computer department. He came home one day talking about the "information superhighway" and how everyone would soon be doing their Christmas shopping from home.

"Really?" I said, not quite believing it. "That's so Jetsons."

I soon went from not knowing what the Internet was to obtaining an e-mail address. Still, during my first few years in the parish, my reliance on Internet communication was minimal. I began to use e-mail and helped develop the church website.

Now, I depend so heavily on the Internet that I could not do my daily work without it. And things are expanding even more rapidly. Every church needs a website, and educational resources are increasingly coming in the form of blogs, podcasts, webinars, and social networking sites. I try to stay on top of such developments, yet these changes continue to happen so quickly that I often feel I'm many miles away from the cutting edge.

Pastors, churches, and religious organizations do not get as much face time with the people among whom we minister. We have fewer sacred moments in the living room and our pastoral visits have been cut short. Yet, the longing for communication, for connection, for intimacy persists as strongly as ever. So, church leaders need to reframe our communications. While we might be constrained from face-to-face communications, we can learn to enhance them with interface communications. But this must be done carefully, never forgetting the sacred significance of flesh-and-blood community.

Today, communication between pastors and parishioners no longer occurs chiefly through spoken word—or even through letters and newsletters. More often, it takes place as people use computers to respond to one another. The forms of communication are evolving rapidly from e-mails, to text messaging, to social networking sites—and we are not sure what might be on the horizon.

It would be easy for seasoned church leaders to be irritated by these new developments. We could throw up our hands and assume all this is for the young; that it's too complicated for most of us to comprehend. I've heard pastors protest, "Are we going to be spending so much time handcuffed to our computers that it keeps us from *real* ministry?"

Even though it feels like an either-or proposition—as if we must choose to spend time with either our church community or the computer—it is not. When I consider the carefully crafted e-mails about deep pastoral issues that appear in my inbox in the middle of the night, I know we cannot ignore the radical changes of the last ten years, nor can we disregard the evolutions in the years to come. Time on the computer is real ministry.

Technology as Social Medium and Ministry Tool

Before I go any further, let me acknowledge that, yes, I do mourn the fact that I spend more days in ministry looking at a lifeless, flat computer screen than I do at the beautiful complexities of the faces in my community. I realize how much I am missing. Yet the need to minister in our current reality is more compelling than nostalgia. Moreover, I've often been thankful a parishioner had a keyboard and screen to "talk" to late at night. At times the Web becomes a needed lifeline for depressed or anxious friends.

As a pastor to college students, I watch the amazing speed at which undergraduates text-message each other. They don't even need to look down as their nimble thumbs race over their tiny cell-phone keyboards. As I see young professionals tapping out messages on their iPhones during worship services, I'm reminded that I need to keep on top of the shifts. (My colleague, John Wimberly, and I often dream of more useful pews that have holders for coffee cups and PDAs.)

The shift—as impersonal as it sounds, and as removed as it is from our complicated and rich facial landscapes—can be strangely intimate. Last year, I presided over a wedding for two people who got to know each other over the Internet while working on a political campaign. Their minds met long before their bodies did. Many couples in our congregation meet through social media or dating sites. In fact, I know many single pastors who rely on Internet dating sites to meet people.

I'm tangled up in a tight web of people right now. I have gotten to know them through e-mails, blogs, and social networking sites. I know what they ate for breakfast this morning and what's going on in their lives from day to day. I could easily pick each of them out of a crowd because I have seen so many photos of them and their families—although I have never met them in the flesh.

This new form of intimacy has developed as the capacity and availability of the Internet has evolved. We are in the midst of a third wave of Internet communications. The first was for military defense. The second included one-way websites, commerce, and e-mail. The third wave (also called Web 2.0) is interactive. It allows the reader of a website to talk back, discuss, and question. It encourages ratings on purchased products. And, most importantly, this wave allows communities to form across continents, and even around the globe, as networks of people no longer have to be in geographic proximity to interact.[2]

The keyboard has become an extension of our minds.[3] It has changed not only the ways we communicate and form community but also the means by which we organize and protest.[4] It has transformed our expectations of power.[5] In our mainline churches, it has allowed a generation to become much more active and connected to our denominations and spiritual communities.

Internet Communication and Context

My eight-year-old daughter and I were walking to a local diner recently. Every Wednesday night, the two of us have a "Girls' Night Out." Though Calla has been sufficiently adventurous to visit the sushi place that serves its food on a conveyor belt, usually she prefers to walk to someplace nearby.

As we're crossing the busy road, my daughter looks up and asks, "Why is the sky blue?" I look up at the cloudless evening. It is still and beautiful weather, and the sky is a serene azure.

Now that Calla is in third grade, her questions have gotten smarter. When she was two, it was easy, but not now. Before I could think of something poetic like, "That particular blue is the color of peace, and when we look up into the sky, it is a reminder that we are to live in peace with ourselves and one another." Or something playful like, "Because it's God's favorite color." Yet I can tell from her tone and her serious expression that she wants to know the scientific reason—and I don't know it.

"I'll let you know in a few minutes," I answer. We get to the diner, slide into the cushy booths, and I pull out mama's little helper. In my purse, I have an iPhone that connects to the Internet. I tap in "why sky blue," press the Google button, and almost immediately have in the palm of my hand an encyclopedia full of answers. I survey them quickly and relay the most satisfying one to my curious daughter.

I wonder what moms did before Google. That moment in the diner makes me realize how much things have changed, especially as the Internet has become ubiquitous. I used to visit my computer for an hour or so every day, catching up on e-mails. It was a station in my house. I needed a sizeable office to house the screen, hard drive, and printer. The computer remained segregated in our living space and in our lives.

Now I have a laptop small enough to carry just about everywhere. And when I don't have that, I have an iPhone on which I can check my e-mail and surf the Web. In other words, the Internet went from a place I'd visit briefly once a day to a resource I hold in my pocket and look at constantly.[6] I use it for maps to drive around the city, the state, or the country. I use it to keep my calendar organized and to remind me of birthdays. I use it for my address book and for movie and restaurant recommendations. I use it to read the endless chatter, status updates, and streams of consciousness pouring from my friends. And I rarely enter a church or business before looking up its website.

The Web is woven into nearly every part of my life. I no longer look up my favorite sites just once, in hopes of finding stagnant information, but check them multiple times a week. Savvy organizations realize this, so they no longer post information as if it were a flat sign that will stand until the paint fades. Rather, sites are full of active, revolving conversations. They are places where we meet people and engage in frivolous chats or meaningful thought.

The pulsing, moving conversation of the Internet is also changing commerce as it allows developing areas to gain new sources of income. It transforms activism by encouraging new ways of informing and organizing people. And it has reformed religion, as the like-minded no longer have to be in single place in order to connect with one another. Constellations form over vast miles, and we can remain in contact even when we are not in the same place at the same time.

This fact was made very clear to me last summer. In July and August, many in our congregation set off for their holidays, and our weekly attendance falls to about half of its total during the rest of the year. This happened again last summer, as it does each year. But we could not help noticing something was different. People who were on vacation in places far away were downloading our sermon podcasts online. In fact, more people downloaded our sermons than were in attendance at our Sunday services.

Our church is growing beyond its walls. People now tell me they listen to the sermons on their commute. They feel a part of the community, even if they are not able to be there physically. Rather than decreasing attendance (as some had feared), the podcasts are drawing people into the church. I have found myself counseling college students on the other side of the country, because they found our sermons on iTunes in moments when they were searching for spiritual direction.

Of course, the idea of a virtual community leaves us with a lot of questions. Can we be the body of Christ without being physically present to one another? Can we love one another if we've never met? Can we appreciate the image of God through the Internet? Can people who listen to sermons on iPods while commuting to their various workplaces truly form a community that serves and cares for one another? Can a church be a church without celebrating the sacraments together?

Probably the answer to many of those questions is no. Yet something is happening, and I believe God's Spirit is moving in these changes. We are reaching beyond, out to our city, our country, and our world in new ways. Like-minded people who may never have met in person are exchanging ideas and information. Pastors are starting online worshiping communities. Social activism and social justice have new ears and a new voice.

Our current generation expects the church to be technologically savvy. Now that wireless service is readily accessible and many people have computers that fit on their laps, or even in their pockets, there is an assumption that vital churches will have dynamic and ever-changing websites that are prepared for more than the occasional visitor checking on church location or service times. Churches can now create an online culture, with blogs and social networking sites.

Even though the Internet has unsavory aspects to it, the benefits far outweigh the risks. Computers are often the best way to contact new visitors, inform our groups, or send supportive messages. Facebook and Twitter have become important ways for congregations to stay in contact with people who move away from the local area or spend much of their time on the road.

Let's take quick look at two primary avenues through which the church can minister in this new day: blogs and social networking sites.

Blogs

The word *blog* is short for *weblog*. Initially, most blogs were like online diaries, but they quickly expanded in scope and subject matter. Today, blogs run the gamut from huge political or sports sites that reach thousands to travelogues or family scrapbooks intended for just a handful of readers. The number of blogging sites multiplies daily.

The real difference between blogging and traditional printed media is that a blog is as much about the conversation that follows a particular posted article or entry as it is about the article itself. Imagine that letters to the editor did not appear in the next monthly issue of a magazine but rather a few moments after the article was published. And people could respond to the letter a few moments after that. The dynamic allows a subject to be explored more deeply and invites many experts into the conversation.

While blogging is sometimes characterized as a shallow medium, I have found that a good blog can generate twenty pages of thoughtful responses and interactions from a wide range of important perspectives. The reader can end up with a discussion that could not have been orchestrated by an editor.

Just as the blog is as much about the comments as it is about the post, it is also about the community that forms. I learned this when I began my blog. At first, only two or three people would visit the site each day. And then more. In a short time, there were several hundred people regularly visiting and reading the random thoughts I would bang out each morning as I drank my coffee.

After about six months, an even stranger thing occurred. While reading the comments and daily thoughts that came in response to what I'd written, I began to get to know people. On a weekly basis, I received calls and e-mails from men and women, seminary students and pastors. A strange virtual community formed. I'd begin to say something like, "My friend, Karen . . ." but then I would stop and wonder, *Is she really my friend? I've never actually met her.*

Yet, there was no doubt about it. I was becoming a part of a network of Christian leaders, a community that had frequent disagreements, inspiring discussions, and even more excitement and passion. I became involved in a group where it no longer mattered how big your church was or how many famous people sat in the pews. No one was checking resumes; instead, seminarians, authors, and pastors of every caliber began talking to one another. Friendships were forming across political and theological lines. And we began to listen to one another in ways that had often felt impossible during our traditional denominational meetings. We started to organize around common causes and to influence one another. We discussed a little bit of theology, reflected on current events, shared helpful resources, and talked through many of the particular challenges of being a minister.

After months of discussion, I shared a cup of coffee with one of these pastors who lives in a town near me. We are worlds apart in our theological views, yet we found many commonalities in our everyday blog posts. When we first spoke face-to-face, I felt as if I were running into old friend. And we both felt thankful we were able to get to know one another apart from the theological silos that would normally separate us.

Blogs can have many applications for congregations and leaders. When used effectively, blogs can invite sermon feedback, resource sharing, or professional support. Learning the art of hosting in the blogosphere is an important ministry tool to develop, especially when we reach out in a new generation that so often uses the Internet and social networking.

Social Networking Sites

Facebook is a social networking site that anyone over age thirteen can join. It functions almost like a giant online scrapbook in which users develop their own pages where they can talk about favorite movies or music, upload photos of family or friends, or offer regular updates about activities and interests. The scrapbook has millions of pages from people all over the world, but most pages can be viewed only by the "friends" of the owner.

When I first joined Facebook, I filled in some information on my own page, then searched for other people I knew who were part of the network and asked them to be "friends." One by one, each person accepted or rejected my friendship request. Soon, I had a constellation of friends who shared their online scrapbooks of literary preferences, family pictures, and party invitations. Colleagues played trivia and word games. Plus, each person has a status line, which says things like, "I'm starting my vacation today. Hooray!"

Facebook is not the only social networking site. Others include MySpace, Twitter, LinkedIn, and Ning—and more seem to be developing all the time, each with different capabilities. There are also worshiping communities on Second Life, a virtual world where people can socialize and connect. By the time you read this book, Facebook may no longer be the most popular site; right now, it is the most useful for our discussion since so many people use the network actively.

Sites like Facebook offer individuals and organizations an important opportunity to relate information, create community, and reach out to others. Churches and denominations can use Facebook to inform people of events, post information, and send invitations to their network. It can also be used to raise money and awareness for certain causes. In my denomination, the Presbyterian Church (USA), a couple of people started a group on Facebook called, "We Need a Young Adult Moderator."[7] The group grew quickly as people from all generations decided it would be good if our denomination elected a moderator under the age of forty. The excitement flourished too, as different people asked to be commissioners for the denominational gathering, and we began to see a much-needed interest in denominational leadership.

News that Bruce Reyes-Chow was standing for the position ran through the Facebook and blogs. Throughout the online constellation of clergy and laypeople, we talked about the possibility and organized ways to make it happen—and Bruce was elected as moderator that year.

On a personal level, social media can provide a community of support in a complex and difficult career. For pastors, social networking provides a source of connection, a place where you can find out what members of your church are up to, or where your colleagues in ministry have landed.

Some sites allow for deep discussions about important issues. For instance, Susan Olson created the Young Women's Clergy Project and set up a password-protected social networking site on Ning, where women clergy under age forty can talk about the joys and frustrations of ministry. Individuals can get support and advice from other pastors in similar situations. Since the site is open only to young clergywomen, there is a certain amount of freedom to struggle with tough issues without the concern of it ruining one's professional career.

Dangers and Downsides

The possibilities in this new age are fascinating, yet there are dangers that come with the increased use of Internet as a primary form of communication. As we form relationships and community in our churches, we will have to be sure our care does not become impersonal. We all know how frustrating it is to call a utility company and spend forty-five minutes on the phone, waiting to speak with a human being. The company tries to reassure us with soothing Muzak and the hypnotic message, "Your call is *very* important to us. Please continue to hold." But the real message is clear: Your call is not all that important to them. If it were really important, they would hire more people to answer the phones.

Likewise, as pastors and church leaders, if we have a website link that invites people to share prayer requests, but the e-mail is not directed to a person or is never answered by anyone, we can be giving the same message. Not only do we need to be attentive to eliminating dead-end links, but we also need to be careful with e-mail as we rely more and more on this impersonal means of communication.

We can too easily rely on e-mails to send sensitive information, or our e-mails can come off as abrupt or even rude. Or, even worse, the technology allows us to avoid complaints that we need to be handling. We can go without answering e-mail because we are not looking at people face-to-face, and so just avoid communicating.

We also need to be very aware of how quickly misinformation and rumors can spread on the Internet. The story of Beth Sentell, a wonderful, gifted pastor in Louisiana, offers another important reminder about that. Beth and her colleague Daniel Hignight carefully led their two struggling congregations through a process of merger. Anyone who has been through something like this knows how difficult it is to combine two entirely different congregations, with distinct cultures, traditions, and leadership structures. Yet Beth and Daniel carefully imagined a way for the two troubled churches to thrive as one congregation.

For the merger to work financially, they needed to begin worshiping together in one church building and sell the property where the other church had been located. The sale took months, and the longer it took, the more nervous they became. Then, finally, they received their first viable offer. The bid was at the asking price, and the buyers—an Islamic Community Center—had solid credit. According to the good laws of our country, it would have been discrimination to turn down the deal. The relieved congregation happily accepted the offer, and the two churches began their rich and vital life together.

Several months later, a conservative independent newspaper of the Presbyterian Church took the story and ran with it. They misreported the facts, saying the congregation had turned down solid offers from other churches so they could sell the property to the Muslim group. Subsequently, anti-Muslim blogs picked up the story and posted it on the Internet. And now, whenever Beth conducts an Internet search on her name, one of the first things that pops up is this story, with all its misinformation and false accusations that her church discriminated against other Christians.

Daniel Solove, an associate professor at George Washington University Law School, writes about the Internet in his book, *The Future of Reputation*. His work has some very interesting implications for seminarians, pastors, and church leaders.

Solove points out the tension between protecting free speech on one hand and protecting reputations on the other.[8] Bloggers are, of course, free to write stories about themselves and post them on the Internet. But since their lives intersect with other people, this means information gets posted about other private citizens and is easily accessible and searchable for years. This is fine, except when a blogger posts ugly or false rumors about another person. The blogger might have no credibility whatsoever, but when that person looks for a job and an employer does a Google search on her, the employer may find questionable material. Rather than digging more to find out if the material is accurate, the employer may simply set that application to the side. The person has been slandered, her reputation tainted.

This affects church leaders in numerous ways. There are people who intentionally try to sully the reputations of pastors. "Heresy hunters" scour the Internet. They may object to women serving in pastoral ministry and call those who do demeaning names. When they disagree with something a pastor or church leader has written on a blog, that person gets publicly attacked. I know one blogging pastor who had an anonymous comment appear on his site, accusing him of being a pedophile. Luckily, he caught it quickly and easily edited it, but people have been called names on pages that they could not edit. I've been vehemently criticized by someone who claimed to be a pastor, but when I tried to look up the address or telephone number of his church, I found no evidence of its existence. These attackers are often funded by organizations or individuals outside of our denominations, but their sites look reputable and their slander can do considerable damage to a pastor's reputation.

Of course, it's not just stuff other people do that can get pastors into trouble. We all want to be authentic and honest, yet most of us have what Mike Yaconelli called a "messy spirituality."[9] We may want to write about questions we are struggling with, yet our jobs often hinge on our reputations. Plus, none of us were born pastors. We may have done some things when we were younger that we've left behind and would rather not recall, yet that won't stop a photo or story from showing up on someone else's blog.

People in their twenties and thirties are referred to as "Generation Google," because so much of their lives has been chronicled on the Internet.[10] A whole host of information is available on us with one search. A potential employer might see social networking pages with photos of partying college days, or other things that a person wouldn't want to attach to his or her resume. Solove notes that older generations may shudder to see such information posted publicly, even if they have engaged in the same behaviors. A young law student in our congregation told me about a friend who was called into a law office for a job interview, and then confronted by several stern lawyers who placed several printed pages from her Facebook site in front of her and said, "You need to explain this, and this, and this."[11]

The Hidden Face

At its worst, the perception of anonymity the Internet offers can lead to what Philip Zimbardo refers to as "dehumanization."[12] In his book, *The Lucifer Effect*, Zimbardo, the researcher who conducted the Stanford Prison Experiment, studied the effects of anonymity in torture (or, as he terms it, *deindividuation*). He found that when people's identities were masked, they were more prone to act out violently. Whether it was a woman shocking another woman in a clinical situation, men destroying an abandoned car, or children playing aggressive games while wearing Halloween costumes, when their identities were obscured, people became more cruel and destructive. Zimbardo also explains that the reverse is also true, that people tend to see cruel behavior as entertainment if the one being tortured is masked—a phenomenon he terms the "Mardi Gras effect."[13] He explains that was how Lynndie England conceived that the torture in Abu Ghraib was just "fun and games."

We can easily see how Zimbardo's research affects interface communications. On the Internet, with identities masked, there is the possibility of becoming entertained by behavior one would not become involved in if it required face-to-face interaction. Hateful speech, rank with bigotry or misogyny, can poison our interactions. The Internet has fueled detestable racist behavior. Pornography and abuse are there, allowing anyone to slip into the space with a mask on. As church leaders, we know this can have devastating effects on families, especially in this time when it has never been so easy to feed and conceal a sexual addiction.

I do not bring these things up to shock or scare us out of using the Internet altogether. I expect that our networks will be vital places for us to communicate and form community. But we do need to be able to discern between good and evil with this seed of possibilities. We need to be aware and careful of the consequences.

Of course, throughout this conversation, there is another problem that we need to remember. We will need to keep in mind all of the people who are left out of this social phenomenon altogether.

The Digital Divide

Right now, in my community of Arlington, Virginia, people line up outside the library early each morning so that they can spend a few moments on the Internet before work. I see them huddled in front of every available screen. The economy is receding and people have been cutting back on the extras, like newspapers and Web access.

Ministering in Louisiana, I was often in contact with children and teenagers who did not have the resources for a computer or Internet access, and they were getting farther and farther behind in our technological society. I have gone through times when I did not have access to the Internet because of the cost. Luckily, I could easily catch up with the advances once I was able to get back online, but it is not always so easy for everyone. The divide is real and it is great, and it calls for responsible handling.

In our congregations, this digital divide is often not only between the rich and the poor, but also between the old and the young. I know pastors who do not allow people without Internet access into church leadership positions. They simply feel such access is a necessity to lead in a twenty-first-century church.

I have never been able to go that far. We have people on our church staff and in key positions of lay leadership who are past retirement age. They do not use e-mail or own computers, but their gifts far outweigh that inconvenience. Instead, we usually have someone who works closely with the people who do not have access, making sure they are not left out of any central communication of the church.

Reframing Communication

In spite of its dangers and the divide, being a part of the online conversation is an advantage for many of us. In the years to come, as our congregations shift, as we engage a younger generation of members who are more conversant with technology and used to the ubiquitous nature of the Internet, then the network may become more of an expectation. Right now, this is a wonderful opportunity for us to reach out. We can engage in the dynamic conversation, learn to use new tools to connect in a new time.

We can be encouraged by people like @Virtual_Abbey on Twitter, who leads men and women in prayer over a Twitter feed. Every evening, I can settle down to a few lines from the *New Zealand Book of Prayer,* typed out in 140 characters, and realize my supplications arise with many around the country and the world.

We can learn from people like Kimberly Knight, who has the position "Circuit Rider." Kimberly does a great deal of online and hands-on networking for the Beatitudes Society, but before she started at the Society, Kimberly planted Koinonia Fellowship, an online community in Second Life, a virtual world where people go to connect, socialize, and create. Neal Locke followed Kimberly's model when he planted 1PCSL, the First Presbyterian Church in Second Life.

The possibilities in this creative and exciting time may very well be endless, and it will be important for our denominations to realize and welcome many of the shifts that occur. As church leaders, we are venturing into an exciting new territory, with so many rewards and a few risks as well. As we begin to journey out, may we do so realizing how much our interface communications may not replace but can enhance our face-to-face community.

I learned this in my work with Bruce Reyes-Chow, the Presbyterian pastor I mentioned earlier who was elected moderator of the denomination. Bruce and I had only met a couple of times when he asked if I wanted to start a podcast. I did, and so we gathered with four other people—Landon Whitsitt, Mark Smith, Brian Merritt, and Heather Scott—to put the show together. Brian is my husband, so I knew him well, but I had only talked to Landon briefly and never met Mark or Heather. And yet, through social media, we began to work together on a podcast called *God Complex Radio*. Not only did we form relationships with one another, but we also became a part of a larger conversation that includes scholars, writers, church leaders, and listeners. Through Facebook, Twitter, a blog, and the podcast, we are gathering friends, forming community, and igniting conversation.

"When it comes to the role of technology in my ministry," Bruce explains, "it is invaluable in staying connected to the folks I serve. The use of technology in my pastoral life is not simply a method of convenience, but it is a genuine acknowledgment of a way of being that is not judged but embraced." As the Internet becomes an extension of our social lives, as its presence becomes an ever-present reality in our world, we must learn how to embrace the tools and the people of a new generation.

The Epiphany of the Face

Finally, as our interactions increasingly move from face-to-face to interface, we should keep in mind that we may be losing something vital in this shift. In *Blink*, Malcolm Gladwell examined how people can often instinctually tell if someone is honest, simply by looking at his or her face.[14] We have learned to navigate, with varying degrees of skill, a complicated map of muscles. Research has shown what poker players have always known: Certain people can read faces. People who have been abused as children are particularly adept at quickly identifying the glimpse of anger or frustration.

Yet our technology limits this ability. The emoticons we use do not make up for the rich and complex landscape our faces provide. Not being able to access the face in our communication blocks us from a river of important information. And it is not just information that we miss; there is something more than that.

The Jewish philosopher Emanuel Levinas writes beautifully about the epiphany of the face. While it is in our nature to grasp for things and to consume them, Levinas explains that when we look at a face, we learn to honor "the other."[15] He uses the story of Jacob and Esau to illustrate this. Remember Jacob, the "grabber," who seized his brother's heel on the way out of the womb and never quit scheming for Esau's inheritance? With help from his conniving mom, Jacob's insatiable need to consume even led him to deceive his very own father on his deathbed. But Jacob's moment of redemption occurs when Jacob and Esau reunite, and Jacob says, "to see your face is like seeing the face of God" (Gen. 33:10).

Emanuel Levinas speaks of this moment as the epiphany of the face. It was as if Jacob saw Esau for the very first time, because he wasn't trying to figure out what he could get from his brother or how he could subsume his brother's position in the family. Instead, he saw God in his brother's face.

We risk losing this epiphany when we move from spending long afternoons over coffee in the living room to typing out short, precise e-mails on our computers. We lose that sacred reminder that each of us is made in the image of God.

As we navigate ministry in a new generation, as we increasingly interface, we do well to remember the importance of our everyday, face-to-face epiphanies and to think of our interface conversations as enhancing rather than replacing them.

chapter 4

Retelling the Message

Church leaders often focus on the possibilities of technological mediums, but they forget something equally important: The message itself is as vital as the medium. The tools can help gather us together, but they will not be effective in building community and inspiring activism unless we understand how to use these platforms to tell our stories.

How do stories bind communities together? How do these small glimpses into one another's lives allow for deeper connection? Though many people who are on the outside of the evolution of social media might see it as a self-absorbed exercise of needless exhibitionism, others engaged in it notice an interconnection forming through the pictures and updates.[1] The medium makes the communication possible, but the message that pulses and reverberates throughout these social networks is made up of narratives. We realize that even as new modes of communication evolve, the narratives themselves are a part of a much longer yet ever-evolving tradition.

In 1940, a man named Jacob Lawrence took all the tales he'd heard about his family and friends moving from the South and constructed a giant illustrated timeline. Collecting both personal stories and information from his local library, he assembled his family's chronology and, with it, the larger story of the migration of African-Americans from the South to the North of the United States.

I saw Lawrence's timeline, sixty-eight years later. The vibrant brushstrokes revived history for me. All the stories Lawrence had heard from family members about the reasons they'd moved were clearly articulated on the canvases. He told of the harsh conditions in the South and what his friends and family found in the North. From one canvas to the next, he drew us into the migration with him, and I understood that important piece of our history as a nation more deeply than ever before.

At the end of the exhibit, people were invited to tell their own stories of migration. I typed out my short narrative of having moved from southern Louisiana a decade ago because I was not able to find a pastoral position at a church that could pay the minimum salary. I had to move north as well, to a climate more open to a pastor who looked like me.

My struggles certainly cannot be compared with those who were loosed from the bonds of slavery. But the exercise of telling the account of my own journey northward helped me realize the deep chord Lawrence's narrative had struck within me.

Personal narratives put flesh and bone on historic facts. Stories introduce the "other" by inviting us to enter into the experience of someone else through her imagination. Stories allow the reader to become captivated by the other, to enter the other's reality. The listener forgets about herself for a moment, until something within her cries out: *That's like me.* Then a connection is made, a connection through emotion and empathy.

The best journalists, sociologists, environmentalists, and other bearers of fact and information often present their ideas within the warm, comfortable robe of a story. This gives the reader not only the details of a situation but also a setting in which to imagine it. She has a chance to smell, touch, taste, and listen to the information, and with those base senses engaged, she is more able to connect with the raw data, and more likely to remember it.[2] The same dynamics are true in our congregations. Narrative is important for creating change, communicating faith, and building community.

Creating Change

Bob tried to quit drinking several times. Most of his attempts were half-hearted—promises he made to himself during the nauseous haze of the morning after. At one point he abstained for several months, going cold turkey with pure, individual willpower. He resumed drinking, though, when he decided to catch up with an old friend over a pint of beer.

It was not until he began attending Alcoholics Anonymous meetings that he was able to stop drinking for an extended period of time. Hearing the stories of suffering, support, and celebration from others who'd battled the same problem allowed Bob to rely on a higher power, depend on an extended community, and commit to change. There is much in the healing steps of support groups that fosters change in a person's life, but certainly the commitment to gather and tell and listen to stories, to mourn and to laugh with one another is central to the program. In fact, Bob relied on the gatherings so much, he knew he needed to attend at least two to three meetings every week to maintain his sobriety.

Support groups like AA remind us that change often happens when men and women have the courage to voice their narratives, to confess that their lives have become unmanageable, and to surrender to a higher power. The words that are repeated ritually in the meetings—from the greetings, to the clichés, to the serenity prayer, to the twelve steps—create community as well as change in each individual's life.

We see similar things happening in our congregations as the vital rituals of prayer, meditation, celebration, and storytelling create change. Renewal can take place when men and women are able to unearth the memories that have been buried and construct an image of themselves as children of God. The power of the words, especially as we share stories together, allows us to gather and to experience transformation on a personal and communal level.

The Power of Words

How do stories create change? How do the words we speak construct a different reality? Our worship is often centered on the expectation that our words will change things. Our liturgies remind us of invisible realities that may not be clear in our ordinary lives but become apparent when we gather together. We, as people of God, often pray—and we expect lives to change and heal.

But how could we possibly expect to see change simply because the people of God have uttered a desire for it? Of course, it is through the Holy Spirit, who works through our communities. Yet we also know that God uses words and stories in that work.

I am reminded of the power of words each night. At 8:00 each evening, I tuck my daughter into bed, and we select a book from her library. Cozy in the bottom bunk, we open the pages and something amazing happens with that flat, black and white text. The words we read aloud build a world in our midst: Orphans survive on their own in a land of no conclusions. A boy travels in a giant peach. Sacrificial love is stronger magic than the power of evil. Goblins, hobbits, and phoenixes are commonplace. Plants come alive; the most ferocious beasts talk. Within the pages, with the help of the author, we visit these realms; we are inspired and shaped by them.

It is a reflection of the fact that we are made in God's image that these imaginary lands can exist between us, that we can create shadow worlds with our letters. For as God's creations, we also create. It is not just the imaginary world that is fashioned by words as a child grows up, but the words we utter in our spiritual communities can signify important realities. We are people of the Word, and the Word of God still moves us, inspires us, and forms us.

For instance, Scripture reminds us that we have the power to bless and to curse (Gen. 12:3). This may seem like a foreign concept, but any father who hears the words "I love you" from his child knows the power of a blessing. The words create a reality. Parents also often have the power to bless and curse, and indeed we parents are typically the first ones to create our children's realities. Our answers to their question of "Who do you say that I am?" have a lasting effect on them, for better or worse. When children are formed under the constant drone of disparaging words, it can damage them for their entire lives. Whether disparaging or affirming, others' words form our attitudes, shape our ability to trust, and model for us how to give and receive love.

We are a storied people. Our lives are formed by the truths and lies we've been told throughout our years. When a mother tells her daughter she needs to lose weight, even when the daughter is completely healthy, that story sticks with her and often haunts her as she looks in the mirror. When a father tells her she's just like her great aunt in her ability to make everyone feel at ease with her humor, it connects her to a long tradition.

In the same way, as people of the Word, Christians are connected through words to a larger history and tradition. In the story of creation, we recall how God created out of nothing, through the use of words: "Let there be light." And there was light. The words formed and created us, separated the dry land from the crashing oceans. The Word then became the history of a people. As the story unfolds, we read of the fiery and comforting words of the prophets. Words are eaten. Words blacken the mouth. Words become as sweet as honey. Words are set in stone and carried around in a dramatic covenantal ark. They are lost and they are found.

Then, we read how Jesus Christ, the Word made flesh, dwelt among us. Over the centuries, as the church formed and continues to form, the Word becomes central to our lives. We read the Scriptures and its stories form our lives. We say and hear, "This cup is the new covenant," and we know these words signify a new reality, a new relationship of promise, forgiveness, and reconciliation. Through those words, we learn we are children of God, and we grow into deeper community with one another. Through sharing the cup, through our words and our teachings, we come to understand we are the body of Christ—and learn to live out of that reality.

When we pour the water of baptism over a sweet infant and promise to guide that child in the faith of Jesus Christ, we know we have entered into a new relationship with her. We have become a part of her, and she a part of us through those waters that connect us also to a long history of saints who have gone before us.

All of these words bind us to a story, a purpose, a community; they form us as they inform us. Most of us never grow out of that longing to listen and be shaped. Even though we live in a culture rich with visual images, sound bites, and advertising slogans, we do not always have a chance to hear unfettered words. We do not always have a chance to connect, on that basic level, with stories and with one another.

Perhaps it is for this reason that story has gained a new significance in this postmodern generation—and with it, many traditional forms of worship and liturgy have found new resonance. Along with the technological advances that connect us, the shared narratives create a transformation as well. Through our stories, the words of change and hope we utter can have the ability to create reformation.

Throughout the Internet, we produce and consume a proliferation of words. And many bloggers, full of blessing and cursing, have begun to dream of change in the church. Throughout the past few years, we have seen how their yearnings have created community and begun to power a transformation. We have yet to understand the full outcome, but we already notice in these discussions the desire and will to start new churches. It becomes easy to imagine how a new community, and its yearning for change, will reframe hope in a new generation.

Communicating Faith

It is not just our own individual stories that are finding new life in this amazing proliferation of words. Throughout our congregations, this renewed emphasis on the power of stories is changing the way we read, hear, and understand God's word in the biblical text and how we reach out.

NARRATIVE UNDERSTANDING OF THE BIBLE

As church leaders, we know that creating and telling stories is an important precursor to change. Narratives are also vital as we inspire our congregations through understanding and preaching the text.

In his book *A Whole New Mind,* Daniel Pink suggests that one reason stories have assumed increasing importance is because facts are so ubiquitous and nearly free now. Whereas we once needed researchers to dig up each piece of information from expansive libraries, the Internet and reliable search engines have placed the facts at our fingertips, making them less valuable to us. In light of this shift, what we really need are people who can present those facts within a context and with an emotional impact.[3]

Growing up in a scientific world, we often assumed the importance of fact over fiction and quickly learn to put away our storybooks. We gave preference to the provable over the mysterious. If it couldn't be demonstrated in a laboratory, it couldn't possibly be true. The rational, logical, reasonable facts ruled our lives.

Yet these facts can rarely explain our deepest desires, needs, and behaviors. They do not fully explain the tenderness we feel for our lover, the strange ways we spend our money, or the vocational choices that pastors make. Truth cannot always be tested and established in a laboratory, human behavior is rarely logical, and the Holy Spirit is often best explained through mystical stories.

In modernity, the world of scientific rationality mingled with the biblical texts and theology in awkward ways. Some people laughed at the scientific inaccuracies found amid the stories. Brushing aside the words, they assumed we'd evolved past our need for fairy tales like God. But I welcome many people into my office who were atheists or had atheist parents, and have spent their lives feeling as if they were missing something. Parts of the biblical story may make no rational sense, but it is a story they are longing to hear.

Some liberal theologians, seeking to be faithful to both the text and modern scientific realities, have explained in great length how the miracles actually occurred. They clarified the parting of the Red Sea, the virgin birth, Jesus's healings, and the resurrection, providing great comfort to many people who found in these insights a way to keep their faith in the midst of our rational world.

Others tried to make the Bible into a scientific textbook. They believed that if the Bible contained any inaccuracies or errors, scientific or otherwise, then the very nature of God would be questioned. And so they attempted to make science bow and bend to the pages of the Bible. Even in the midst of amazing findings and fossils, they believed the world was created in six twenty-four hour days, roughly six thousand years ago. Such beliefs were often coupled with contentions that women ought to be subject to the rule and authority of men and that the Rapture would be occurring any moment now.

The awkward conversation between the text and science continues and has been highly politicized through battles between those who favor evolution versus creationism, feminism versus gender complementarianism, and the sanctity of heterosexual marriage versus same-gender relationships. We see heated debates over school textbooks and religious arguments about what should be taught in the classroom. For those who hold to a literal interpretation, even biblical prophecies—the predictions of future events—have found a place in forming foreign policy.

Yet in the midst of our rational world, something else has grown up. It is the truth and power of the Word that cannot be proven, cannot be tested, and cannot be photographed. It is the humble knowledge that the Scriptures speak of things that go beyond historical facts and chronological timelines. The Bible offers narratives that form our lives. Its words are so often visible reminders of invisible realities. They have the power to shape us as they move through our collective unconscious.[4]

We understand and respect the fact that the Bible was not written in an age of science and technology. The genre is different, yet that does not take away the power and truth of the biblical story.[5]

In the modern age, scientific realities ruled much of our lives, and rightly so. Yet mere facts leave us longing for something else. In a new generation, we are fascinated by the untested, the mythology that forms us and shapes us. There is creative, mysterious, and spiritual power in words that leaves us yearning for stories to be heard and to be told—stories that surpass all understanding yet somehow guard our hearts and minds. The power and importance of the story in communicating faith should not only be acknowledged as we read the texts but also as we preach them.

Preaching the Text in a Postmodern World

I learned to preach while on an internship with the Anglican Church in Uganda, Africa. Navigating orange dusty roads from village to village in a Land Rover, I would preach several times a week. Although I'd taken classes in homiletics, none of the reference materials I was taught to rely on were available in these rural villages of eastern Africa. But, I was there, moving around beautiful people, singing new songs, learning new dances, and hearing so much through their stories.

As my preaching voice formed in this rich and beautiful culture, I began to craft narratives. With a Bible in hand, I learned to pick out the words from the text that challenged or confused me the most. As I wrestled with the Scripture, I would spend much of my sermon preparation time in the mud-hut kitchen. Sorting the tiny stones out of the beans and rice, I listened to the women of the village laugh and tell stories. Drawing from the verses and the Ugandan culture, I learned to write narrative sermons that sat alongside the ancient texts. The stories built bridges of understanding between our cultures and the Bible.

After seminary, I became the pastor of a small Cajun congregation in South Louisiana. By then I'd collected a solid theological library, and I did extensive research in preparation for my sermons. Yet I still came up with stories. Maybe I was inspired by something in the water, because Louisiana is a wonderful place for narratives to unfold. As I drove through the swamps, I realized I was in the company of Walker Percy, Tennessee Williams, Kate Chopin, and Earnest Gaines. Like most Cajuns, the members of our congregation relished a well-crafted narrative and used beautiful metaphors to describe even the most mundane days. When a cold morning greeted us with a light dusting of snow, they would say, "It looks like the baker and his wife got into a fight last night!"

When my daughter was born, I learned that the placenta needed to be buried under a large oak so my daughter would grow up big and strong; that my infant needed to wear a hat because robust winds would give her an earache; and that there are a hundred ways to alleviate the pain of teething. I heard predictions that "she was a girl with muscadine eyes, so she would marry a boy with eyes of sky blue."

The sense of timing in Louisiana had nothing to do with a clock on the wall. Instead, it had to do with how long a story needed to be to make sure the punch line delivered the right impact. It was a culture where metaphors were embraced and shared, and where tall tales and good music were always part of the entertainment. It is no wonder that many great writers have come from the swamps of Louisiana.

Since these are the places where I formed my preaching voice, my sermons are often woven into a narrative. The art of telling a good story continues to be important as we keep preaching in a new generation. The stories told in the pulpit allow other people to reimagine their own narratives. They give us a chance to connect to one another and to remember we are bound to a common history, and they give people something to remember when they leave the sanctuary.

Often, we are taught how to dig up the facts surrounding our lectionary, but we do not always learn how to set our interpretation within a context and imbue it with emotion. Yet we can learn to create a culture of storytelling within our churches. As that happens, we will have a powerful tool as we reach out to our neighbors.

Reaching Out

The business world has discovered that a narrative is the best sort of marketing tool. New companies like StoryQuest have developed in order to help businesses identify and harvest the stories people tell and tie them to the larger mission of their corporations. Businesses are also learning the art of blogging as a way of sharing their stories with a larger audience, and they are realizing the importance of reviews as well.

These innovative business models should be no surprise to those of us in the church; they are simply reinventing the long-standing wisdom of Christianity. In congregations, we have used testimonies to reach out and spread the good news for thousands of years. And in a new generation, we evangelize in much the same way we always have. It is just that our culture has a renewed interest in narrative, and we have more tools to spread the word.

How do we reach out in a new generation? Evangelism does not come easily for most of us. When we think of the "e" word, we might imagine tracts of "Four Spiritual Laws," wily street preachers, tacky Christian broadcasting, or uncomfortable family dinners. And yet, the heart of sharing the good news is simply telling one's story—letting friends know what happened in our life and how our community of faith helped. Reaching out begins with the practice of testimony, of sharing our lives with one another, and being fluent in talking about our spiritual journeys. When we initiate this vital discipline, we learn to speak more fluidly about spiritual things to the world around us.

In developing the art of storytelling within our faith communities, we allow people to put words around the movement of God in our lives. Most often, this craft is best taught by modeling it. In other words, as church leaders become more comfortable with talking about God in their lives, their congregations will become more adept at using the language.

Church leaders are privileged to hear different narratives, and some of the deepest moments in our faith communities occur when people begin to recognize the spiritual struggles in their lives and put them into words. They take these resonant insights, they identify those points where their lives intersect with God, and they begin to form a vocabulary for those deep stirrings. It's a powerful process.

We might recall the fortune cookie message that sounded a lot like a message from God, the Christmas Eve service that moved us to tears, or a wonderful mentor who affected our life. We all have these experiences of the Holy, but we rarely get a chance to talk about them. One of the most sacred things we can do as people of faith is to share the story of our lives, look back, and reflect. Often we do not see God at work unless we look into the rearview mirror. Until we have the chance to tell our stories, we may not realize how all the right roads converge so beautifully, or how the rough, uneven patches form us.

By verbalizing our stories within our congregations, it becomes easier to share them also with our wider community. As we practice the art of telling these accounts, we become comfortable with our spiritual journey. When we have a vocabulary to describe that path, the Word becomes flesh and dwells among us, moving about the people.

Strangely, our mainline Protestant culture sometimes seems less fluent in spiritual language than the dominant culture. Many of us have been taught not to mention religion in polite company; yet the members of our political parties, characters on our televisions, and artists in our pop culture speak easily of their spiritual lives. As a result, many people are turning to Oprah rather than the churches for spiritual guidance.

As church leaders listen to the stories within our congregations, we become aware of the larger, corporate narratives that emerge. Church leaders can be careful as we craft these narratives with honesty and optimism. Our congregation's ability to communicate openness and care in the midst of spiritual questions and doubts is vital as we reach out in a new generation.

It is easy for our churches and denominations to slip into a narrative of decline, which leads us to impart a message of deprivation: Come to our church because we need more people, money, and energy (which doesn't sound like good news at all). If we want to reach out to a new generation, we must avoid communicating that we're seeking just another warm body in the pew, another giving unit to meet the budget, or more volunteers for our programs.

Yet, if our churches can develop and communicate a narrative that invites people to enter—if they are places where a person can slip into the pew for an hour of internal wrestling, where she can mentally question everything that happens, and at the end of it, she knows that such questioning is okay—then people will attend again. Because, after all, we often talk about the spiritual journey as a matter of acceptance, but in reality it has more to do with struggle. Then, after a good long time, if she's willing to listen to the stories of the community, her own story will begin to form in her belly. It's an extensive, tough, and beautiful process. And it is one of the great things about being church.

Oddly enough, it also brings us right back to where we started this chapter—considering the way new media technologies are shaping the way we tell "the old, old story."

Building Community

"Writing down my Facebook status is always a moment of introspection for me," a clergy friend told me recently. "You know, I have to ask myself, *What am I doing?* It makes me reflect on my life."[6] We agreed that Facebook updates are a form of testimony—maybe not the full-blown sharing of God's work in our lives, but opportunities that make us ruminate on the mundane, seek out salient moments, and form tribes through those small words.

I believe the popularity of Twitter speaks to the function of story in our culture. Twitter is a site where people write brief (fewer than 140 characters) updates about what they are doing and receive similar updates from other people. Refreshing the posts by computer or cell phone, people reply to one another's short memos, and then the narrator's voice becomes engaged in dialogue. As I follow the regressive chronological time line from my friends' tiny posts, I get snapshots of their lives. They tell me about their days, and I tell them about mine. We share the diminutive details of changing diapers, pastoring churches, and writing dissertations, and we mark the huge transitions like moving across the country or getting married. Our stories weave in and out; sometimes we write about matters we have in common (like elections, liturgical seasons, or celebrity deaths), and other times we jot down personal things. Through all of it, I hear testimony. People may be sharing their most mundane and piecemeal frustrations, but their stories build over the course of the disjointed updates. The small fragments, taken together, compose the stories of our lives.

We no longer gather in the evenings on the porch to snap field peas, pull the silks off the corn, and enjoy the evening air as my grandmother did as a child. Most people are busy with office work in the daytime, and when they arrive home in the evening, they might keep up with the national news and sports. The space where we once told our own stories has been diminished in our country and is often replaced by the stories of characters on the flat screen. We no longer compare ourselves with real people but with characters in sitcoms. We see our own stories through the lens of hour-long dramas, shows in which the grief over a death is resolved before the commercial break. Yet our own complicated life problems are rarely resolved in an hour. It is no wonder people in this day are more depressed than ever before.[7]

Since it often takes eighty hours of work instead of forty to support a household, our social lives have been cut short. We are not able to gather with friends or connect through civic organizations as we once did. Our chance to talk to one another has diminished.

Yet in a new generation, an astonishing movement has occurred. In the busyness of our schedules, in our anemic social lives, people are turning off their televisions and they are using flat screens to tell their own stories. Through innovative social media, they now gather together in virtual communities, report on their days, and relate the stories of their lives. Now, through blogs, podcasts, social networking sites, and Twitter, the power of the narrative emerges in new ways, as an amazing proliferation of words arise. Through enterprising mediums, creative messages form and people share stories—and this allows spaces for communities to take shape.[8]

Religious leaders know how the power of a story creates community. Christians have been gathering to share testimonies since the Day of Pentecost. Church members have always known how giving away a bit of oneself and allowing other people in on the story of one's life can increase empathy in a community and can weave a group together with common cares and concerns. What is new, what we are learning now, is how social media can enhance that connection.

Innovative technology allows connections to be made, but having the structure that allows us to build a network is not useful without the content. Perhaps that is one reason why, in this exciting moment, we are watching the revival of the story. Though storytelling is as old as cave paintings, the tradition has taken on a new form and rhythm. While a new generation gives constant account of what they are doing, we see an emergence of the narrative, coming out in a particular way, as it forms communities and inspires change.

chapter 5

Reinventing Activism

I t is difficult to understand the Christian drive for social justice without talking about the reign of God. In a new generation, this outrageous belief continues to compel our activism and remains the substance of our hope. The idea of the reign of God was declared by the prophets and embodied in Jesus. Now the hope reverberates through the Internet. The call for justice takes the form of causes people join on Facebook, digital petitions citizens sign through e-mails, education on vital issues on blogs, and important news echoing through Twitter.[1] In various forms and functions, people of faith are joining together to stimulate our merciful imaginations.

Jesus taught about the reign of God in parables. He sought to wake people up to the longing already growing within us, the deep yearning that there might be peace between enemies and that all people would be fed and sheltered. Jesus taught us to imagine a better world and inspired us to be better people as he spoke of this movement of God that would be a challenge to the status quo.

Even as we long for and work toward the reign of God, it sometimes seems like we know it more by its absence than by its presence. That certain pining reminds me of when I was pregnant and living in South Louisiana where I served as a pastor in a tiny, rural congregation.[2] As many expectant moms do, I had a craving: a particular, powerful yearning for a ripe piece of fruit. The taste of it was almost in my mouth, so strong that it even awakened me from deep sleep and haunted me the next morning.

I wanted something with a thin layer of taut skin and with meat that would burst with deep sweetness and shallow tartness all at the same time. The longing was all the more intense because my body knew it needed something, some sort of vitamin that can only be found there, in that fruit.

I scoured the grocery store, but its offerings were sparse. I missed the rows of rolling produce set up in beautiful patterns I used to find in the city I moved from, that vegetarian heaven of Austin. I would wander for hours through a maze of fruits and vegetables, making new discoveries on each visit. But there, I searched through tabletops of scattered remains, haphazardly thrown together under harsh, buzzing fluorescent lights. Picking through the store's meager offerings, I looked for the right hue, pressed gently, and smelled for that distinctive flavor. I could almost taste it.

Yet when I brought the produce home, it turned out to be hard, colorless, and bland—a pathetic replica of what my body yearned for and needed.

When a man asks Jesus about the kingdom of God and when it's coming, Jesus responds mysteriously: "The kingdom of God isn't coming with things that can be observed. They won't say, 'Look, here it is!' or 'There it is!' For, in fact, the kingdom of God is among you." (Or did he say "within" you? It is hard to translate. Maybe he meant both.)

His are strange words. We cannot see God's reign, yet somehow it is among us. It is as if we know the reign of God best through our deep personal and communal longing for it. We understand what it is because of something within us that needs it and craves it. We can almost taste it.

Walter Rauschenbusch was a pastor who worked in Hell's Kitchen in New York City at the turn of the twentieth century—a time when the neighborhood's title was apt. He became impassioned by the poverty and struggles of the people around him. A hunger grew inside of him, and so he wrote that the kingdom of God reminds us that Christianity is "a great revolutionary movement, pledged to change the world as-it-is into the world as-it-ought-to-be."[3]

Rauschenbusch is part of a chorus of Christians who cry out with longing. He stands alongside John the Baptist, who wildly calls for repentance. He preaches with Martin Luther King Jr. who tells of his dream at the march for jobs and freedom. He joins with Dorothy Day and the Catholic Worker in the house of hospitality. And he gives voice to that hunger within us—a craving to be fed as well as to feed one another.

We look at our communities and yearn for the moment when the homeless will obtain shelter and the abused will find sanctuary. We see our nation and dream of a day when the sick will receive care. We look at the world and ache for the era when wars will cease. We long to see the time when the brutal economic forces that push certain nations into more and more debt will be held back. We pray, "on earth as it is in heaven," until the hunger grows up within us so that nothing will stop us from working to that end.

And there it is: The reign of God. We can point to it, we know it so intimately that its sweetness is almost on our tongues, but we cannot quite realize it. When we're consumed by the world-as-it-ought-to-be, that great revolutionary movement when the presence of God's reign becomes powerful in its absence, then we know the reign of God is somehow within us and among us.

The idea of the reign or kingdom of God has been used in different ways throughout our history. It has been a utopian vision for settlers establishing a new world; it has been a battle cry for wars; and it has been a promise held until after you die.

Now, it is being recognized once again in our hope for our world to be different. Right here and now, we are longing for wars to cease and for peace to reign. We are praying for a world in which each and every person is fed and sheltered. We see the great inequities, and we know we can do a better job caring for one another. We realize that each person is made in the image of God and has dignity and worth, no matter what his or her earning potential is. The requirements of justice, mercy, and humility ring true for us.

The longing bursts all around us: People like Shane Claiborne and others in the New Monastic movement seek the reign of God through communal living and reaching out to their neighbors; Brian McLaren writes that *Everything Must Change*; Eric Elnes voices his concern for social justice and a progressive faith that resonates through our generation; Sara Miles compels us to feed one another, through both her writing and her own work serving the hungry in San Francisco; and Julie Clawson teaches us how to "do justice" everyday.[4] Each new voice that springs up points to that hunger that is in us and among us.

All of us in our different ways are reframing our longing for the establishment of God's reign among us. What is deepening this longing for justice in a new generation? What sorts of changes are taking place in our attitudes? And how are we taking up new tools to satisfy this yearning for God's reign?

Globalization and Its (Dis)Contents

Answers to such questions can take us by surprise. Recently I asked a conference participant to explain what it was like for her to be in her twenties. "I am a part of a generation that has all the information in the world, literally at our fingertips."

"Yes!" I responded with great enthusiasm. "Isn't it amazing?"

"Well, sort of," she shrugged, and halfheartedly and politely gave in to my eagerness, "but mostly it's just really scary. *We have all the information in the world at our fingertips.*" When she repeated the statement, the gravity of it touched me. She was pointing out that while it is wonderful not to have to go to the library for every bit of information, there is a burden in having that knowledge. Her generation is growing up knowing all about wars, starvation, and huge inequities among people all over the world. No wonder our hunger for social justice is so acute.

Her remark reminded me of the short-term mission trips I took part in as a teenager. A lot of concerns have been raised about these trips, and important questions have been asked about whether they do any good for the people who are receiving the guests.[5] The journeys cost a lot of money, and some wonder if those resources might be put to better use in other ways.

Whether or not the excursions were more than mere tourism, they affected my life deeply. Digging up sewage pipes in Switzerland, stripping wallpaper in France, sleeping on a houseboat in Hong Kong, meeting Christians in China, leveling ground in the Philippines, and preaching throughout Uganda, I gained a tremendous perspective on the world and on different cultures.

My experience is common. In addition to the Internet's offering an increased awareness of events happening all over the world, many U.S Christians of my generation have traveled to other countries, helped churches with manual labor, and worked alongside other Christians. Along with the inevitable culture shock, we brought home with us a hunger for social justice and lingering guilt about how much we consume.

I remember packing up my clothes and other possessions for my trip home from Uganda, Africa, and having a certain hatred for all of the stuff that I owned. At that point, all my material possessions could fit into a studio apartment, but I still felt regret about them. I wanted to give away all my shirts and skirts to the people who surrounded me and needed them much more than I did. I donated as much as I could, but still realized I needed a lot of clothes to make it in our culture. The inequities between the haves and the have-nots of our global economy felt crushing.

By contrast, previous generations often had more limited awareness of the situation in other parts of the world. As a child, my mother was told to eat her dinner because children in China were starving; yet she found it difficult to make the connection. "What do those children have to do with my potatoes?" she would wonder. Now, we fully understand that other children go to bed hungry—we may even have met some of these children—but we just do not know what to do about it. We want to share our full plates, but we're not sure how. We are replete with food, but a deeper hunger to right the injustices remains.

Here in the United States, buying things is often a hobby for us, a way to show appreciation for loved ones, or something we do to cheer ourselves up when we're feeling down. Yet as we look at all the stuff piled up in our attics and garages and see our children's overflowing toy boxes, we wonder how it grew so quickly. We are concerned that we consume too much, from the plastic bags we carry home from the grocery store to the Styrofoam peanuts in which we drown our Christmas gifts before mailing them. We know the earth has become exhausted trying to keep up with our demands, and we worry about the environmental damage that we cause. We end up with the feeling of dread familiar to people preparing for postretirement downsizing:

our shame builds as we sort through all of our stuff and realize how much we have that we don't ever use let alone need. Often, we have a lingering self-hatred that can overwhelm us.

We understand the discontent and frustration this new kind of globalism introduces in developing countries, as people in these countries gain access to television and the Internet, and suddenly can glimpse U.S. lifestyles and feel the fury of the great inequities.[6] However, affluent Christians in the United States often encounter a different kind of frustration. It is the vexation that comes to those who should be content in our globalization. We can feel trapped in a cycle of consumption and disheartened by huge inequities, yet we do not quite know how to get out of it.

Our information-overloaded generation is aware of the huge disconnect between the lifestyles of many U.S. teenagers, where high school proms are a $17 billion industry, and the lives of the many other teenagers in our country and abroad, who do not have even basic food, clothing, or shelter for the day. We hold PTA fundraisers so our children can go on yet another field trip, while many other parents are trying to make sure their children get one meal a day. We recognize outrageous absurdities; for instance, the amount of money spent on bottled water is three times the amount it would take to solve our global water crisis.[7]

U.S. church leaders who have worked with different people around the world recognize how our wealth has come at the expense of others. Through travel and Internet access, we have increasing experience with the suffering and excesses of the global community and know our systems of consumption are broken. All this ignites within us that longing for the reign of God, that dream of each person being fed and sheltered.

With this increased knowledge comes a heightened sense of responsibility.[8] It is part of the epiphany of the face: when we come face-to-face with another human being in need, we see God in that person, we understand we are traveling together, and we are compelled to reach out to her.

One of the greatest gifts our churches can pass along to a new generation is our long tradition of commitment to social justice that is best encapsulated in this notion of the reign of God. This hope can become a cure for our information-immersed cynicism. If our strong vision of what God intends life to be like could team up with the leadership and innovation of a new generation, this could be an amazing time for our congregations and our world.

Reframing Activism

That is, *if* we could team up. But the fact is that there is often a subtle yet persistent ageism in our movements fighting against sexism, racism, and homophobia. People who actively protested in the 1960s wonder why the young men and women of today do not have the same passion they had. Some older feminists chide younger women for not giving them enough respect for what they've accomplished. Younger activists become frustrated with older leaders whom they perceive as so trapped in a habit of reminiscing about past successes that they forget to look at the pressing needs of today. The boards and chief executives of many nonprofit and social change organizations are drawn from a strong network of people who are *all* over the age of sixty.

Unfortunately, long-time activists sometimes neglect their responsibility to mentor young leaders and often prefer not to share power. Younger generations have little tolerance for being trapped into "us against them" patterns, yet they often feel Boomer idealism is soaking in it. For many young adults, pragmatism determines partnerships. For instance, if younger progressive Christians can partner with more conservative evangelicals to help care for creation, they will—even if the evangelicals have different views on same-gender rights. But then, younger generations can fall into setting up "us against them" patterns with older generations.

This shift in attitudes and the lack of younger leadership in many longstanding groups often causes the new generation to begin new initiatives rather than team up with those who have gone before them. Though the birth of new movements is promising, problems arise because these initiatives can run out of steam and dissolve quickly. While established organizations need innovation, vision, and a younger demographic in their constituency, younger organizations need relationships, wisdom, and a stronger network of support.

The biggest divide can come with the tools of the new activists who are increasingly Internet savvy and dependent. Some view Twitter as a ridiculous waste of time and do not value Facebook as an educational resource. While most activists rely heavily on e-mail now, they might cast aside other tools of social media. Unfortunately, when established organizations reject new technology, they not only dismiss effective and inexpensive tools, they can also rebuff a new generation's way of life.

What is our alternative? What are some possible ways we can use these new tools? Let me give you a couple of examples.

Implementing New Tools

"Half of our annual income came from Twitter, either directly or indirectly," Hugh Hollowell, the director of Love Wins explained to me. Love Wins is an organization that provides unconditional love and relationship to chronically homeless and very poor men and women. Hugh is a friend and a chaplain to people on the streets of Raleigh, North Carolina, providing hospital visits and pastoral care. Many people know of Hugh's work primarily through his effective network building on Twitter.

I was also reminded of effective social media use when I received, for the fourth time, an invitation to join the cause "Not For Sale" on Facebook. The first couple of times I got the invitation, I didn't really understand the organization. I assumed it had something to do with rejecting rampant consumerism in the United States. But in response to this fourth invitation (which, like the others, came from a friend who knows my commitments), I visited the website and learned more about the problem of modern-day slavery. This led me to delve deeper into issues of human trafficking, and as I did I realized that Not For Sale (NFS) is using current technology to empower and equip a new generation of activists.

I wondered how it all developed, so I bought the book *Not for Sale*, and I spoke to the author David Batstone about how a book turned into a movement.[9] David told me about how he'd read in his local paper that one of his favorite restaurants had been trafficking women from India to work in the kitchen. When he realized this could happen in his own backyard, he was shocked, but that shock quickly grew into a resolve and an active passion. David began to travel all over the world, learning about the problem, recording the stories, and meeting abolitionist heroes. Now the Not For Sale campaign works to stop human trafficking in several different ways, as the activists work to stitch together a global movement. They work with law-enforcement officials, faith communities, corporations, consumers, and all sorts of justice seekers to fight modern-day slavery.

Not For Sale has a website that acts as a hub for the many things they do. They have a cause page on Facebook; they engage with Twitter. They produce *The Underground,* a weekly e-zine. They have an interactive slavery map, where people report on human trafficking in their own locations. "We use a lot of cutting edge tools," David explained to me. "We're right in the backyard of Silicon Valley so we can even talk to the CEOs of these companies to find out how to get the most out of the technologies." David said that when he speaks at an event, he tells listeners that if they have only one minute to contribute to the movement to end human trafficking, then they need to sign up for the Facebook cause. "Everybody laughs," he told me, "but it really matters." Because there were so many people who were a part of the cause, David was invited to speak to all the employees of Facebook, and UStream broadcast that speech to its three million subscribers. The leverage of social media helped to spread the message about ending human trafficking, which is extremely important because this injustice grows when no one sheds light on it.

When I asked David how the technology was used most effectively, he explained that whether it is a church or a social-justice group, it comes back to the story. "The most important thing is the bigger story, the narrative, the hero's journey. To communicate that well, you use a range of media platforms. You can use traditional media. Then you can ask about your Twitter strategy and your Facebook strategy."

I also spoke to Allison Trowbridge, Not for Sale's national director of communications, and she explained the tremendous growth of the movement since it launched in 2007. "We are able to scale everything we do. What we put out as an organization reaches many more people than direct communication would allow." She explained that twenty years ago, she would have put stamps on thousands of envelopes and sent information out to the mailing list. Now she can update the website from anywhere in the world, sending out bulk e-mails, Facebook messages, and Tweet news. The report goes out to NFS's friends and followers, who can then forward and retweet it to a much larger audience. Law enforcement is sensitive to public opinion, and when there is an outcry about something, they are more likely to respond.

The technology also helps the organization work directly with law enforcement. On the website, there is a slavery map with closed cases of human trafficking. But there is also a confidential map where NFS can upload tips they receive of trafficking all over the world. Then, they can work with law-enforcement officials to help stop trafficking.

"The problem of modern slavery is such a dark and heavy subject," Allison explained. "Through all of this, we're able to offer a bit of light and a story of hope."

Hope is being reframed. Activism—the work that springs out of a desire for peace, the longing for justice, the cry for freedom, and the yearning that all will be fed and sheltered—has been renewed in the prayers and the politics of a new time. We can see it as our understanding of God's reign deepens, the effects of increased globalization weigh upon us, and innovative tools for organizing activism develop.

These new ways of mobilizing for peace and social justice come at a time when public protests seem bigger than ever but also less effective than ever. People become frustrated when they march for peace and a handful of participants begin destroying property, and the message of the entire gathering is disregarded because the headlines focus on the violence rather than the original intent of the demonstration. Or if there is no violence, giant protests occur, and the media does not seem to notice that they happened at all.

The marches and sit-ins of the Vietnam War and Civil Rights era were protests that both wreaked havoc and provoked positive change. Yet those forms of protest are no longer gaining much notice. It is up to this new generation to find innovative means of protest and activism that are effective in this new era.

The religious community is just beginning to catch on to the possibilities. The power to organize, without the huge cost of an organization, is becoming clear to many Christians who want their voices heard on issues like stopping wars, preventing poverty, deterring homelessness, providing health care, and protecting the environment. Information and updates can be sent over the Internet quickly without the burdensome expense of mailing, and Web recruiting can accompany and support our face-to-face efforts. Now we can easily gather around an idea or cause, invite our friends to join us, and have a movement—just as David Batstone has done with Not For Sale.

Hope and activism are being reframed. An old hunger for the reign of God is taking on new vitality as we use new tools to reach out, inform, and connect with a new generation. If we can appreciate the insights and innovation that a new generation brings to us, if we can acknowledge their passion and commitment, if we can navigate these cultural and technological movements and appreciate the possibilities that are there, then our activism can be renewed—and can be a force for renewal.

chapter 6

Renewing Creation

I am walking in the woods, as I so often do. Or, at least I like to imagine this place as woods, though it is actually just a small patch of green space that follows a stream, a "run" that flows right through the homes in my neighborhood. Walking and praying is my main spiritual practice, a discipline that helps me gain a sense of clarity I rarely find anywhere else.

Often, when I begin to walk, all I can hear are the buzzing arguments in my mind. My head is racing, still caught up in the last complaints or criticisms I had to manage. But as I continue, my attitude changes. I glance down, hearing the crunching ground beneath me and listening to the steady rhythm beneath by feet. Then, suddenly, I notice the birds singing. I look up and begin to think of things beyond my little world. I begin to pray and ask God to lead me. I begin to pray for other people. Noticing things in the trees, like the scurrying chipmunks and the floating butterflies, I'm reminded that I am part of something larger than myself, and I feel more complete. Staring at the pulsing streams, I find peace and healing.

On one particular walk, after strolling for about a mile, I arrived at a clearing near a private college. Stepping into the bright sunlight, I noticed two deer close by, a mother and her baby. The deer seem all the more amazing in a neighborhood where most of the animals I notice are domesticated or rodents.

I stand transfixed. It feels almost as if I have intruded upon them, stepping right into the middle of their dining room. Now I can't help but watch the family enjoying their meal together. After I've watched for a few moments, admiring how the doe perceptively leads and the fawn gently nudges, my eyes meet the mother's. She continues to chew casually, but I freeze, feeling like a caught spy. They are not startled in the least; they are majestic and peaceful, and seem perfectly comfortable with me being there.

Before long, another person walks down the path. A young college student, with earbuds resting on either side of her head and a small MP3 player in the palm of her hand, is using the trail as a shortcut from the library to her home. As I watch her walk toward me, I expect she'll notice the marvelous creatures standing just a few feet away from us, but she never does. As she passes me, I reach out and touch her on the arm, and point. She looks up, completely startled. With her mouth wide open, she tugs on the ear buds until they fall from her ears, and then tucks them into the pocket of her jacket. We stand there as still as statues, taking in the beautiful scene.

"I can't believe it. And I almost missed it," she whispers to me as we part ways.

That moment in time typifies our current milieu. We often forget to look around us. We rush from one place to the next, connected to entertainment, music, Wifi, and wires all the time. We process a constant stream of information.

It makes sense. The way we live reflects our professions. Over time, our country's economy has shifted from an agrarian-based system, where a large percentage of the population were farmers who tended the land, to an industrialized culture where many people manufactured products, to a technological and service industry where the market rewards ideas and innovation. It was once obvious to us that our survival was connected to the seasons and the health of the earth. Today, for many of us, it has become a matter of survival to stay in tune with the many innovative changes.

Just as our economic focus has shifted from the soil, our whole lives have followed. We no longer feel bound to the well-being of the ground the way we once were; at least, we are not always aware of the immediate connection between the earth's health and our own. We are so captivated by human production that we tend to forget God's creation.

Becoming Attentive

As children and adults, we have become detached from our earth, unaware of what happens around us. Our air is conditioned, cool enough in the summer and hot enough in the winter, so we do not worry about the weather too much. The humming of appliances surrounds us and devices sing out dissonant chords constantly so that we cannot hear the sweet melody of the birds.[1] Concerned that our kids might become bored, we've packed their days with activities, so they no longer enjoy long hours imagining the animals that the cumulus clouds form and watching the grass grow.[2] We have chased our children with Purell bottles so tenaciously that they no longer make mud pies, yet nonetheless are more susceptible to disease.[3]

Even though we have grown oblivious to the earth, the words of Romans never seemed so true: Creation is groaning, because it has been subject to much futility. And the creation is waiting for the children of God; it is waiting to be set free from its bondage of decay (8:19–21).

The earth's groans have become louder and louder. We hear the reports of global climate change and are admitting its catastrophic effects on our lives as well as the entire ecosystem on which we depend. As we learn about the devastating effects of the oil disaster in the Gulf of Mexico, we have become aware that we are on a trajectory toward destruction. With rising oil prices, we are slowly waking up to the reality of our limited natural resources. The rapid development of China and India from agrarian to industrialized economies means their populations are moving into the middle class and into big cities. This upward mobility will result in many more people buying cars and relying less on bicycles. The global effect will be an increased strain on the earth's resources, more rapid climate change, and the realization of even more destructive habits.[4]

As gas prices continue on their roller-coaster ride, their lurching and climbing moves across our country, affecting the prices of food and other necessities. Families who were already living on tight budgets are finding the increased costs difficult to handle. After a decade-long bigger-is-better vehicle trend, we are unable to pay for the petroleum such vehicles demand. We are trying to get rid of our gas-guzzling SUVs, and suddenly small, economical hybrid cars are looking more attractive.

Our global consumption patterns loom so large that it can seem beyond our ability to do anything about them. The inevitable crisis feels too big for us to handle. To change our ways, we will need every imaginative resource we can muster from religion, science, literature, economics, business, technology, and the arts.

What are our churches doing to respond to the situation? In our liturgy, preaching, and practice, we too often reflect our larger world in the ways that we distance ourselves from creation. Our congregations gather in mighty fortresses that keep us comfortable in all sorts of climates. In fact, many churches spend a fortune keeping their sanctuaries at a certain temperature all week long so that their organs and pianos stay in tune. Too often, we sing about the glory of God's handiwork and then gather for coffee served in Styrofoam cups. Our children are confused by the pastoral parables of Jesus because imagery of seeds and soil is so foreign to them. Even if our membership shrinks until we only take up four of the forty pews in our sanctuary, we cannot imagine moving into a smaller, more sustainable worship space.

We interpret the biblical creation story to perpetuate the notion that humans have "dominion" over the earth, and we construe that to mean any and all of the earth's resources are there to be consumed for our economic gain. Indeed, in this highly politicized milieu, the dominant Christian view in our culture is often presented by the Religious Right, who contend that exploiting the environment for economic development represents faithful stewardship of the resources God has entrusted to us. Creation is seen solely for consumption for human need and purposes, and there is an idea that the resources of the earth will keep renewing themselves for our profit.[5] Furthermore, in some evangelical corners, there is a lurking notion that both human life and the earth on which it depends are transient and what really matters is our eternal life and salvation, so there is less concern about caring for our environment here and now.

Yet, in a new generation, it is becoming difficult for us to insulate ourselves from the groanings and ignore our abuse of the earth. Even in our sterile, interior comfort, we realize that something will have to change drastically, very soon. We recognize clear witness against unbridled consumption in the Bible. Our tradition beckons us to be caretakers of the earth, and it instructs us to take a Sabbath—time off for our soil and ourselves. A Christian way of life teaches us to refrain from consuming twenty-four hours a day, seven days a week, never allowing our bodies or our planet a time for rest. That one simple act of adopting a biblical approach by allowing one-seventh of our time for respite would begin much-needed restoration for creation, including ourselves.

The voices of theologians and preachers calling us to environmental stewardship are getting louder in a new generation. Many congregations have found how we can reframe hope by caring for creation in our individual and communal lives. Congregational leaders are pointing out the truth that we are a part of creation, and if God has granted us a role of power over the earth, then it means our responsibility to care for the ground, water, and air is heightened.

It's become clear when I speak to my friends, especially those younger than me, that there is a shift in attitude, an urgency that could not be detected years ago. In fact, 94 percent of adults born after 1978 agree that "our country must take extreme measures now, before it is too late, to protect the environment and begin to reverse the damage we have done."[6] Since environmentalism is such a significant issue in a new generation, many people are attracted to spiritual communities that make creation care a priority.

During the coffee hour at our congregation, I've often heard people explain that they attend our church because all of our energy comes from wind-power. We still have a long way to go, but we are realizing that a renewed dedication to the environment not only helps the earth but also attracts new members and helps our church.

If our congregations could become a source of renewal and education when it comes to creation care, then we could have a major impact on global issues. Through our teaching, our land usage, and our care of the earth, our churches could become centers of hope whose practice and mindset ripple far beyond our walls to our community and to the world. As we think about the number of Christians around the globe, and how much land we own collectively, imagine what a significant effect we could have.

In vibrant communities of faith, we can often see a philosophical, emotional, and practical approach to caring for the earth. All of these strategies function together as we build a sense of care in our worshiping communities, as we work for an embodied faith and a grounded spirituality.

Embodied Faith

Most of us are aware of the damage our lifestyles have caused to our environment. We've heard what scientists are reporting about the causes and effects of global climate change. We realize what will happen in the years to come if we do not change our ways. But like the addict who clutches her cigarettes even though the doctor says they are killing her, we have not been able to alter our behavior enough. Why is that?

It is because changing our lives takes more than scientific facts, logical arguments, or economic considerations. For many people, deep sustaining change can come only from a spiritual decision.[7] While science and the church have too often been on opposite sides when it comes to matters of the environment, we are beginning to realize that an interdisciplinary approach to this problem is vitally important. We cannot separate the spiritual from the scientific any more than we can detach matters of the spirit from concerns of the body. We need an embodied faith, one that upholds the material and the spiritual aspects of our lives and appreciates how these two aspects work together.

Our culture often sees science as much more important than religion and spirituality. Science is seen as more credible, because its theories can be tested and proven. Religion has no such laboratory, and so it is often relegated to a less important status.[8] At the same time, our religious tradition has a long history of trying to separate the spirit from the body and degrading the material. In the first century, many Christians held to Gnosticism, a sort of dualism that teaches that the spirit is divine and it is trapped in an imperfect material body. The divide between the physical and spiritual world set up an idea that the spirit is of greater importance than our physical selves. And in different forms, this thought has streamed through our faith for centuries.[9]

In our current milieu, many Christians have come to a more holistic understanding of body and spirit. We know physical ailments can affect us spiritually, just as emotional problems can cause inordinate stress and trigger physical problems. What we eat, what we drink, and how much we exercise affects us not only physically but also emotionally *and* spiritually. The spiritual and the material cannot be compartmentalized. Rather than pulling us away from attending to the material, the best spiritual practices invite us to participate in what God is doing in the world.

I have learned to pay attention to what my body is telling me about my life. When I am under too much stress, my eye begins twitching. When I'm avoiding a disagreement with someone close to me, quick jabs of pain shoot through my stomach. When I work too much, my legs tend to ache and exhaustion overcomes me early in the evening. These physical indicators become clues to my spiritual health and wholeness.

The same attentiveness that includes taking care of our souls and our bodies, the spiritual and the material, extends beyond our selves to the air we breathe, the water we drink, and the food we eat—the environment that sustains us. How we take care of the world around us and how much we are in contact with creation have a major role in our spiritual lives. And we learn to nurture creation in important ways in our spiritual communities.

During Lent, many congregations have begun practicing an embodied faith by encouraging participation in a "carbon fast." Instead of just denying our chocolate cravings, we encourage our community to do something that will help care for creation. So, for forty days, we urge the members of our church to turn down their heat, take the bus, eat at home, consume less meat, do without bottled water, or do something else that will help the environment.

This forty-day discipline reminds us that our spiritual practices are not only about prayer and the inner life but also about participating in creation. Furthermore, although we might enter the season of Lent thinking, "I can do this for a short time," these life-giving practices are habit-forming. We become used to wearing the extra sweater around the house, making our family's meals, or relying on public transportation.

As we reframe hope in a new generation, we will continue to build the bridge over the traditional chasm between the physical and the spiritual and learn to become more spiritually grounded.

Nurturing a Grounded Spirituality

George Washington Carver was a botanist and educator who spent many of his years teaching former slaves farming techniques so that they could become self-sufficient. A former slave himself, Carver lived from 1864 to 1943, and in the South he is widely recognized as a man who helped the transition from cotton crops to sweet potatoes and peanuts.[10] The rotation was extremely important for the Southern states, as cotton was being decimated by boll weevils and was depleting the soil of its natural resources.

Carver's influence was not just in agriculture. He was a deeply spiritual man, and in many ways his contributions were as much religious as scientific. He once said, "Anything will give up its secrets if you love it enough"—and that seemed to be his attitude toward nature. Taking a brush and paper, Carver would paint plants, capturing their beauty as well as studying them. He said, "I love to think of nature as an unlimited broadcasting system, through which God speaks to us every hour, if we will only tune in."

Carver is a great inspiration to me and his words often come to my mind as I pray and meditate. I wonder if renewing our love for creation is the key to the spiritual problem that's led to our environmental devastation. We know that studying our physical world can indeed lead us into intense spiritual understandings.[11] I believe an enduring, respectful relationship between science and religion, a grounded spirituality, will be vital to overcome our most difficult environmental problems.

It takes time to nurture a grounded spirituality, yet admiring the creation often leads me into a deeper relationship with the Creator. That's why I enjoy walking so much. It initiates a connection that begins with gratitude and moves quickly and surely to wonder. There are places in my life that are holy, and they are almost always among the jagged rocks, the flowing water, and the fine sand. It is when I examine the detailed texture of each shell that I know we have an amazing Creator. As I look closer and closer at the veins of simple leaves, I begin to get a sense of the majesty and complexity of the earth.

Knowing all that surrounds me settles my anxiety. It helps me to breathe and pray. And it leads me to gain a new appreciation for the Divine. Through walking, I begin to realize God's creative power, and I have a sense that I am a part of that flowing source. What I do affects the earth, and the earth has a deep impact on my life.

People throughout the centuries have seen God in the beauty of creation, but in the past, we have been more tied to nature. It affected us differently when we lived a largely agrarian culture. Since the industrial revolution and the advent of air conditioning, we are less tied to the vagaries of land and climate. And yet, there remains this notion throughout Scripture, throughout our most important spiritual works, and within our own deepest longings that attachment to the earth is vital for our spiritual nourishment. And so the importance of our communities of faith as centers of education, ideas, and modeling becomes apparent as churches realize the importance of nurturing an appreciation for creation. And it begins with our children.

Grounded Children

There was a time when kids in our country spent most of their days outside, playing and exploring for hours until parents would finally make them come in. A love for nature often grew up then, as kids on the beaches explored the varieties of shells and others near the forests climbed into trees and watched birds. Now, there is a concern that children have Nature Deficit Disorder;[12] in fact, 70 percent of children in the United States have a vitamin D deficiency because they do not get fifteen minutes of sunlight each day.[13]

As our economy became industrialized and families became more urbanized, parents were more concerned for their children's safety, and realized it was not always wise to let children run around the neighborhood all day. With two parents working, children have structured after-school activities, and it is often dark before we can take them to the park. Additionally, it seems our survival instincts have evolved; the necessity to understand the earth became replaced by a need to make sense of technology. Parents encourage their children to play on the computer because they know their sons and daughters are more likely to get good jobs if they understand technology.

Yet, things are shifting right now as we realize our survival *will* depend on our children understanding the earth. As we feel the tension from our world's growing thirst for gas and pay the price for wars being fought over oil, many people believe our earth will not be able to handle the growing needs of our global economy, even if we tap every resource available to us. If we continue our current consumption, we know other resources of water, land, and clean air will be in short supply as well. The generation growing up in our congregations will be forced to think about the shortage of natural resources in ways we never have.

What are churches doing to nurture an embodied faith in our children? How are we teaching them to love our Creator and to love and care for the creation? One way is by connecting the stories of our faith to our traditions and our practice.

One congregation here in Washington, DC, The Church of the Pilgrim, has a Vacation Bible School series in which they reflect on creation. Each day, they celebrate communion with the children, using a liturgy based on the first chapter of Genesis. During the prayers, they place a dark cloth on the communion table. They introduce each day of creation by placing on the table glow-in-the-dark stars, a large glass bowl of water, colorful fish in the water, and toy animals on the land. Every morning, they talk about what God created, as they connect creation back to the Sacraments.

Then they extend the lesson to our everyday lives by taking the boys and girls on walks through their urban neighborhood. They encourage the children to point out things they like and dislike about the neighborhood, in order to connect the themes of creation, the Sacraments, and the environment. They move from the narrative of the Scriptures, to the tradition of the Sacraments, to the practice of creation care.

Likewise, our congregation, Western Presbyterian, works to unite our stories, traditions, and practice. We have a summer curriculum in which we teach our children about the importance of water, connecting the waters of baptism with the water of the earth. Beginning with the story of creation, we follow the water as it flows through the Bible— with the great flood, the Red Sea parting, water coming from a rock, and Jesus's baptism. By studying the stories of our faith, we connect with both our own baptisms and our need to preserve this precious resource. As we learn about water as a life-giving force, we also point out that there are many parts of the world where people do not have access to clean water. We show children that responsible stewardship of our world's resources is a Christian spiritual practice.

Moving from the baptismal font to the communion table, we also talk with the kids about bread. We often stress that the table in our sanctuary is connected to tables all over the world, including our tables at home and the ones in Miriam's Kitchen, where we serve a hot, nutritious breakfast and dinner to over two hundred homeless guests each weekday. Knowing that many urban children do not have the chance to grow food, on Earth Day the kids in our church plant an herb garden for Miriam's Kitchen, so the chef can have access to fresh seasonings.

During another summer, the children learned the stories of bread in the Scriptures.[14] Through each lesson, they heard how the people of God were fed, and how they served one another. Learning how manna came from heaven or how a crow fed a prophet led to that sacred moment when Jesus uttered the words, "This is my body." Throughout the stories, we were reminded of how we are fed and how we can feed one another, in times of plenty and of want.

Before World Communion Sunday, we taught children how to make bread, taking care to show them the process from the time the wheat is grown. The kids learned to make different kinds of bread, from kneading the kinds of loaves that they eat at home to rolling out the flat pitas that are enjoyed in the Mediterranean. All during the year, children contribute cereal to Miriam's Kitchen, on Easter they dye eggs for the guests, and on Thanksgiving, they collect fruit for the homeless men and women served there. In each step, as we gather around the different tables in our church, we encourage the children to reflect on the scarcity and abundance of our food, where it comes from and where it goes.

GROUNDED ADULTS

Of course, our congregation's efforts to nurture a more grounded faith do not end with the children. During the same summer when our children were learning about water, the adults in our congregation began a water-bottle pledge, where we committed to avoid the use of disposable plastic water bottles, drink from reusable containers, support public water utilities and affordable access to clean water, and learn more about local and global water concerns.[15] It began when members of our church became frustrated during a park cleanup as they walked along the banks of the Potomac River, filling bag after bag with discarded plastic water bottles. Bending over, collecting each piece of plastic that littered our shores, they started thinking more about our national dependence on bottled water. Taking a closer look at these bottles, they realized petroleum was used to make the containers and gas was burned while moving the water from one place to another. Often, the bottles get recycled—but the cleanup made it obvious that they were not always recycled.

Then an even greater concern sprang up. We know most people in the United States have access to clean drinking water, but what might happen if more affluent people continued to drink bottled water? Would we still care about the quality of our tap water? Would the standards of our public system slip and cause water quality inequities in our country, as there are in so much of the world? Could the bottled water trend lead to unfair availability of one of our most basic, life-giving resources?[16]

We realize that our spiritual practices have bodily implications and we are often looking for ways to care for the earth. To that end, we did the usual things: participated in an energy audit and changed our light bulbs to CFLs. We also helped to revitalize the neighborhood farmers' market. Churches are often in the perfect position to start fresh food markets, because so many of our worshiping communities have the necessary space and parking available. That was our situation. Since we have some space in the basement of our church, we are able to store signs and tables. Now local farmers gather a couple of blocks down, selling fruits and vegetables to DC residents.

It seems like a small thing, but the positive impact on the environment will be big as more churches get involved. When we buy produce from local farmers, it cuts down on the fuel costs from shipping produce from other parts of the country or even the world. Farmers' markets give growers a reason to diversify their crops, creating farming habits that are better for our nation's soil.

Besides providing healthy food for people in the church and community, farmers can also help families who need assistance. Many farmers' markets can accept tokens from food stamp recipients, the elderly poor, and recipients of WIC (Women, Infants, and Children). Oftentimes, calorie-dense food is cheap, filling, and readily available for low-income people. Since our food pantries are stocked with unhealthy items, there is an incentive for people in poverty to eat junk food, which can lead to obesity, diabetes, and heart disease. In contrast, farmers' markets give an incentive for people who need assistance to eat fruits and vegetables that have been picked fresh that morning, leading to better health overall.

In the evening, adults and children from our congregation go to the market with baskets and "glean." Reframing this tradition that is older than Ruth and Boaz, the farmers will donate fruits and vegetables that did not sell that day, and will not be fresh for the next market. The congregational members then take the fresh fruits and vegetables to Miriam's Kitchen.

Many congregations are looking at the connection between our communion tables, home tables, church tables, and environment. At First Presbyterian Church in Tallahassee, Florida, church member Kathleen Engstrom makes pumpernickel bread for communion and the church's Wednesday night dinners. She and her husband, Cal, serve vegetarian meals for their community meal, trying to get all the produce locally. "Primarily we use vegetables, fruit, legumes, berries, and Kathleen's wonderful bread," Cal says. "The response has been very positive; everyone likes simple healthy food."

We see creative churches working and imagining what they can do all over the country. As people of faith are expanding their wonder and hope in the midst of the current crisis, spiritual communities are doing incredible things. Westminster Presbyterian Church in Belleville, Illinois is constructing a community garden so that their neighborhood can begin to eat produce from the land. In urban areas, some churches are even constructing rooftop gardens.

In moving from the narrative to the tradition to the practice, we create a culture within our worshiping communities that extends far beyond the sanctuary walls, inviting people to see their ordinary lives as something sacred. By continuing to nurture a healthy view of creation in our country, by continuing to be innovative in our approach, we are changing the cycle of consumption in some profound ways.

In our churches, care for the creation can lead us into a deeper community. Many congregations are learning this as they host trash-free lunches and coffee hours, making sure all the dishes, napkins, and mugs can be washed and used again. Congregations encourage parishioners to BYOM (Bring Your Own Mug) and other churches form "green teams" who are responsible for the laundry and the dishes after each meal. Washing, folding the laundry, and putting the dishes away can create a renewed sense of mission and solidarity.

I learned something about community when I went on my Lenten carbon fast and gave up my car. The forty days were habit-forming for our family. My husband and I learned to rely on the bus and subway instead. By the end of our time, we decided we did not need a second car and got rid of it.

Now, I admit, it is not always easy. Sometimes, I am not able to rely on the bus, and it can be embarrassing to ask for rides. I don't like to be so dependent on friends. That was the hardest thing to get used to—feeling like I was fifteen again, had lost my independence, and was always having to mooch off of church members. It is humbling to have to ask for a lift, even when the person I'm asking will be going right by my house. Yet, we know community often springs up when there is some mutual dependence. When I do have a car, I am much more aware of people who do not and I offer them rides. And, over time, I've noticed that I rarely have to ask anymore: Church members have formed the habit of offering me a ride themselves.

Ride sharing is a wonderful way to build community. The members of a mosque in our area are learning this. Since mosques are not on every street corner, people tend to drive for miles to get there. Realizing this trend, a local Imam decided to designate the best parking spots around the mosque for carpoolers. They encourage people to seek out other families and travel to worship together.

Imagine what this does for a community of faith, as people begin to look around and see where their neighbors live. They learn who doesn't have a car or doesn't drive for some reason, and they begin to care more deeply not only for their environment but also for one another.

As we look at global climate change and other massive environmental problems before us, our predicament can seem so huge that it feels hopeless. But then we figure out that some of our largest problems can have very small solutions. When we begin to stir our merciful imaginations and think of the possibilities, when our congregations begin to model different behavior, we can have a great effect on how we care for our earth. The answers come as Christians begin to tend to an embodied faith that realizes the importance of science and spirituality; when we can look at the water in the baptismal font, the bread on the communion table, and begin to see the important relationship between our narratives, our traditions, and our practices, then church communities become models of creation care. Our practices of stewardship can radiate from our communities.

Refashioning Our Buildings

In the years to come, as so many things are shifting, as many of our congregations near the end of their life cycles, as we and our denominations begin to imagine the new communities that will spring up, becoming wise with our buildings will be of utmost importance. Our church buildings are often enormous, with high ceilings and air conditioning that was never meant to be. Our sanctuary walls might be covered with beautiful, dark stained glass, but this glass doesn't allow any natural lighting to flow into our worship spaces. Many churches are unable to afford to the double-paned windows, proper insulation, and other measures that would make our heating and cooling systems more earth friendly. The art, architecture, and histories of our buildings make them difficult to leave, but when congregations of less than one hundred are meeting in sanctuaries built for a thousand, we need to rethink the structures. Congregations can deplete themselves putting endless resources into the care and upkeep of an older building.

As older churches close and new congregations are planted, imagine if we were able to employ our finest, most environmental-friendly architects and artists to plan what our worship spaces could be. What if different denominations came together and hired someone to design a beautiful space with natural lighting, using the best of our technology to create something lovely?

In the history of Christianity, congregations often pooled their resources to create grand cathedrals, and those massive structures became our ideal of what a church should look like. What if we came together to create buildings for a new generation? What if we began to imagine structures that were environmentally friendly? We could create plans for adobe sanctuaries, bamboo constructions, and educational buildings with solar panels or community gardens on their rooftops. We can begin to imagine beautiful windows that can let light in and allow air to circulate, rather than depending solely on air conditioning.

The thought and care does not need to stop with the building itself. It can keep going as we walk outside of our doors. Imagine what we could do with our landscaping! Planning gardens with trees and plants native to the area would save money, time, and natural resources. We could plant gardens where bees might thrive.

Churches do not often have the human or monetary resources to keep up with all the changes and innovations. However, the practices of caring for creation can flow easily and naturally from our worshiping communities. When children begin to learn how the narratives of the Bible connect to our Sacraments, when adults think about carpooling to church, when we begin to think of our spaces as a part of God's creation, and when we begin to take care in everything from avoiding the Styrofoam cups to carbon fasting as a spiritual practice, we are reminded that we are stewards, and we allow our faith to become an integral part of our everyday lives.

chapter 7

Retraditioning Spirituality

W hen I was a teenager in the booming evangelical movement of the 1980s, my church often pressured my generation to get rid of all our "secular" music. The local Christian bookstore had comparison charts, instructing customers that if they liked a certain band that got regular radio time, then they would *love* this particular Christian alternative. I was taught that nothing spiritual could be found "in the world"—everything needed to be repackaged with a Christian label so that it would be safe for Christian consumption.

At Christian concerts, musicians often preached homilies between their songs—lamenting the evils of secular rock music, urging us to ask Jesus into our hearts, and beseeching us to buy more albums. We were warned about "backmasking"—how bands were trying to brainwash us with hidden messages. If we played their records backward, we could hear how they were subliminally encouraging us to worship Satan. Heavy metal bands were linked to Hitler. And, there were a myriad of stories to scare us about AIDS (as if we needed anything else to scare us about AIDS!), the standard story being about a fan who got carried away in romance, slept with a guy, and was greeted the next morning with a small black box, with a coffin charm and the words, "Welcome to the world of AIDS."

My faith was formed amid this strange subculture of consumer-driven Christianity. Christians had their own rock music, romance novels, business books, radio stations, television shows, children's cartoons, women's magazines, stationery sets, sport shirts, and breath mints. Virtually every secular product had a Christian counterpart—which was, frankly, a slightly substandard replica of the same item, usually mutated with a pastel coating and stamped with a Scripture verse.

It wasn't that Christian artists were all bad. But they were under considerable pressure from the industry to keep their music, visuals, or writing trendy, free from anything that might be considered questionable, and certainly with a straightforward religious message. Songs about depression or even ordinary struggles were not tolerated unless the problems were quickly resolved with a "Jesus will make it all better" chorus. Musicians who didn't follow the rules of the game were quickly dropped from their labels.

The message was clear to all of us: The products of the world were dangerous; they could not be trusted. Christians must turn their backs on the secular and buy into the religious. Deep dividing lines between the worldly and the heavenly, the secular and the sacred, the body and the soul, the material and the spiritual were set up. With those dichotomies in place, we knew that we were to shun the former and embrace the latter.

Now, if you are in a mainline denominational church today, you might be shaking your head, thinking this was some aberrant cultural thing affecting a small group of teenagers in Florida, and that it has nothing to do with you and your church. But it probably does. For this was happening at a time when our denominational churches were waning. Evangelicalism was the most robust religious movement of the time, and often seemed to be the only one reaching out to youth. Since this alternative Christian subculture affected a large percentage of teenagers who went on to be church leaders, many of the vital church movements of our day formed in response to what happened when our country was in the passionate throes of evangelicalism.

One of the most important responses is the rejection of this alternative world that evangelicalism had established; the strange idea that Christian art should be imitating secular art, and then turning around to say the secular is evil. It did not make sense, and could not hold up very long—especially among people who do not really appreciate having Bible verses stamped on everything they own. Frustrated with the inability to maintain creative freedom, annoyed by low-quality art, and feeling manipulated by the marketing strategies of contemporary evangelicalism, this new generation of Christians began to reject the flimsy claim that our culture is bad and that a muted, religious version of culture is good. We questioned these false dichotomies between the sacred and the ordinary, the spiritual and the material, the soul and the body.

At the same time, a much larger conversation was taking place in the academy over a multitude of polarities. The modernist mindset often understood things in a dualistic manner, with the two poles in constant conflict and competition with each other. Yet new approaches were deconstructing these dichotomies. We were realizing that these flimsy segregations lead to false impressions and a shallow understanding of who people are and how things work.[1] Understanding the United States in terms of red states and blue states might make for an exciting election season, but such dualistic thinking can also color our perspectives about people. It encourages us to make unfair assumptions about who people are and the opinions that they hold. Furthermore, many people question the accuracy of these dualities—especially when it comes to the sacred and the ordinary, the spiritual and material.

The Sacred and the Ordinary

While selling the sacred became big business, some Christians lost any sense of value in common things. Finding God in the ordinary was something I learned in the denominational church, but not as a student in a confirmation class. It was in a much more ordinary way.

I was a janitor in a Presbyterian church long before I joined the denomination. I worked there during one summer break from college.

I remember each Friday morning looking into a closet where they had a calendar that listed the church seasons. After checking the season, I would carefully wash my hands and get out the paraments for Sunday that were neatly hanging over a rod. Most often, the calendar indicated that the day called for green cloths. In the still silence of the sanctuary, I loved touching the emerald brocade, smoothing my fingers over the light texture, and I was fascinated to learn that the church had a season that celebrated Ordinary Time.

"Ordinary Time" refers to *ordo* or numbered time, and it acknowledges the beauty of steady growth, the regular and the routine. As I learned about the season, I began to realize my life was not split into two separate worlds—the sacred and the ordinary. Instead, I began to see holy moments throughout my numbered days, even in my work as a janitor: checking the calendar, unfolding the cloth, setting it on the table, and trying to figure out those ancient symbols that had been embroidered in gold. Understanding the beauty of Ordinary Time opened my eyes to the sacred and the goodness in the world around me. I began to notice it more and more in our society, and the imposed dichotomy of the secular and the sacred evaporated.

Of course, dividing the secular and the sacred can make our jobs easier as church leaders. If people believe they have to be inside a church building to encounter God, then fundraising for a new sanctuary can be much simpler. If people believe that pastors are closer to God, and that God does not speak except through ordained clergy, then our jobs are much more secure. If we don't maintain that divide, then we may not know how to respond when a church member tells us he skipped Sunday services because he feels closer to God on his sailboat.

Yet, when we begin to realize God is present in every moment, in the ordinary growth of numbered days, instead of just the special moments sponsored by the church, then we can see the world in a much different light. We gain a more holistic view of nature, ourselves, others, and God. We can better understand the mingling of the spiritual and the material, and acknowledge God's rich presence permeating every corner of our lives. We can open ourselves to the myriad ways God reveals Godself. Furthermore, we can invite men and women into a vital faith that allows them to think more broadly and theologically about their everyday lives.

Body and Spirit: Presence in a New Generation

What do our everyday lives look like? Often our days are spent looking at a lifeless screen and scrolling through a list of unanswered e-mails. What sort of impact does this have on the way the way we do ministry?

I believe the way many of us inhabit the world is inviting us to re-examine the meaning of presence. In our faith and throughout church history, we have always wrestled with questions about God's presence, whether the specifics had to do with the resurrection, the Eucharist, or icons. The disciple Thomas doubted that Jesus had risen until he could actually touch the wounds. And, we are often left wondering, was it a physical resurrection? If Jesus's physical body was resurrected, how did he suddenly appear in rooms where all the doors were locked? But if it wasn't physical, how did he eat? Why didn't his closest friends recognize him? How did he ascend into heaven? Why did his resurrected body still have the gaping wounds of crucifixion? We ask these questions about physical and spiritual realities.

During the Reformation, there seemed to be constant concern about the physical and spiritual world. As they considered the Eucharist, great minds began to ask important questions. How can Jesus be present at the table, as well as on the right hand of God? In what way is Jesus Christ present? Is Jesus present in our memories? Is he present in the gathered body of Christ, the church? Is Jesus Christ present in the actual bread and wine?

Then there were the iconoclasts—a movement that sought to destroy traditional religious icons. These representations were seen as idols, and the iconoclasts thought people were praying to the paintings or the statues instead of to God. The defenders of the icons—the iconodules—argued that these religious symbols were physical representations of a deeper reality.

As scientific knowledge increased and our ideas about matter and substance began to change, our notions about these realities evolved and became more complex. Now, we are comfortable with the idea of an icon—we click on them every day on our computers, causing a new program to start or a new folder to open. We know that icons are often pictures or a physical representation of something else. And at this point in history, we are wrestling deeply, not only with spiritual and physical presence, but also with virtual presence. We no longer visit a computer for an hour a day, but instead we live with computers in our backpacks and even our pockets, as we stream messages in constant conversation with one another, constructing avatars and profiles. In so doing we create representations of ourselves.

When I was a child, my mother taught me that physical presence takes precedence over technological presence; therefore, I was never allowed to talk on the phone at the dinner table while the family was gathered. Today, my mother routinely answers her cell phone during meals. Co-workers e-mail each other instead of getting up and walking ten feet into the next office. Spouses sometimes ignore their own families so that they can engage with their online communities.

Though we have become accustomed and even addicted to the digital world, we also long for something deeply spiritual and yet also more physical.[2] Now that our virtual lives seem to take up more and more of our time, there can be a growing longing for the landscape of our own souls, guidance from that still, small voice, and the Word that does not cause eye strain.

Digital presence can often deepen our longing for an embodied spirituality. So, as we work as church leaders in a new generation, we can keep learning how to use these technologies in ways that invite and enhance a faith that is fully embodied.

Sometimes we fear that new technologies and the virtual community they help create will make obsolete our need to gather together in the same physical space. For instance, I mentioned earlier that when our church began our sermon podcasts, there was some question about whether people would download them instead of attending services. We worried that men and women would rely on the downloads in lieu of our communal lives together. It did not work that way, however. In fact, our attendance increased. As members of our congregation traveled over the weekend, or they had to miss a Sunday, they did not drop out of the church community completely; rather, they learned to stay in touch by listening to sermons on their iPods during their commutes to work.

When they are spaces where we can seek God together, our gathered communities can be places where many people connect spiritually and can enjoy being together. Postmodern Christians are much more comfortable than modern Christians with the notion of unembodied presence, yet we cannot ignore the longing for human contact and spiritual community.[3] In this digital age, we are still reminded that we need one another, physically and spiritually.

What do the practices of this spiritual/embodied community look like? Churches are learning how important incarnational, or "in the flesh," ministries are. They are also realizing the importance of such practices as walking, breathing, sitting, meditating, and singing. All these things relate to our whole selves: mind, body, and spirit.

Vital Practices

Our Christian churches have not always encouraged an embodied spirituality. Have you ever wondered why so many people who grew up in the rich tradition of Christianity choose to explore other religions when they want to learn how to meditate? What does it say about our churches when so many people declare that they are "spiritual but not religious"? Why are our congregations known more for fighting over ordination standards than for being places where we can learn to open ourselves to the still, small voice of God? In our churches, why are our members more likely to learn how to put together a meeting agenda than they are to learn how to sense the Holy Spirit's movement?

These are all questions that go to the very core of our identity as spiritual communities. These are questions many church leaders ask—and we don't like the answers we hear. The responses leave us with a need to discern our purpose. As a result, we realize that we will have to reframe our lives together as congregations. There is a great deal of interesting work being done in vital spiritual communities, but I want to focus on four particular efforts: practicing prayer, developing intuition, seeking direction, and reordering our lives.

Practicing Prayer

Our communities are learning anew how to practice prayer, in many different forms and disciplines, and especially through drawing out the silences in our lives.

Church leaders are often told that in order to reach out to the image-driven MTV generation of Christians, we need to be flashing photos on big video screens and using PowerPoint in every service. This new generation has an attention span of no more than two seconds, we're told, so we need to keep them entertained at all times in our services. I would never want to disparage the creative innovations that are taking place in many faith communities—from writing interesting new music, creating engaging visual art, and drawing inspiration from their own time and place. Yet I hate for small congregations that cannot afford the flashy images to become frustrated and feel that vital ministry in a new generation is out of their technological and budgetary reach. Because even as many of us put ourselves under considerable strain buying expensive equipment, uploading images, and finding just the right songs, words, and photos to make our services exciting and compelling, members of the MTV generation are leaving our churches, grabbing their mats, and flocking to yoga studios in order to get some peace and quiet.

Does it make sense to create a counterculture that simply imitates culture? I ask this question not as a person who is against popular culture but as someone who has found that church people do not often copy pop culture well, if that is their main intent. We can try to make our music and presentations appealing to a new generation by imitating what they are used to, but there is a growing longing for something else.

For wired women and men, people who live constantly alert to incoming e-mail and flashing images, there is the hope for a bit of time when we might unplug. In this moment, when we are bombarded with so much information, we yearn for the ability to pause, to collect our thoughts, and to remember what is important. As the stock market continues to swell up and burst, and we are losing our jobs, incomes, medical insurance, homes, and material possessions, we long for a place we can gather to remember that wealth and power are not the keys to a happy and whole life. In a milieu where a full calendar reflects a successful and useful person, there is something within us that drives us to rest. In a culture where people are surrounded by sound and images that are masterfully designed to tell us we will never be successful, fulfilled, or satisfied enough unless we consume, there is a longing for spaces that give us time when we can hear ourselves think and we can invite the voice of God.

When we pray, we open ourselves up to an inner life that is free from constant demands and we create a space where we can be reminded of what is significant. Away from the droning messages that continually remind us of how we never have enough and are never good enough, we can take a moment to be thankful for what we have and who we are. We begin to shift our attentions from our own frivolous desires to the deep resounding needs of other people. And through prayer, we can cultivate a connection with a living and loving God, a God who holds us and steadfastly loves us, no matter how well we perform.

Holly learned this as she faced the loss of her job during the recent economic crisis. She'd been working as a counselor for ten years when the stock market tumbled. When the board of her organization studied the budget and tried to make all the line items add up, all of a sudden her duties seemed expendable. At business meetings, she began to hear the same words repeated: "Personnel takes up such a large portion of our operating budget. I don't think that we'll be able to weather this crisis without making some painful cuts." Then she began hearing her name whispered in the hallways while regretful men shook their heads. As the rumors swarmed through the office, it became clear: Holly was about to lose her job.

Holly thought of all the people she'd helped through crises, the community programs she supported, and the close friends with whom she worked. She recounted the sacrifices she'd made for the organization—all the times she worked late into the evening, all the vacation days she neglected to take. She'd made those sacrifices willingly, because she loved her job and believed her work was important. And yet, now that she realized her position was at the whim of a volatile stock market, it seemed like nothing that she'd done had worth any longer.

Without her job, Holly would lose her home and her children's livelihood would be in jeopardy. As she imagined what could happen, her anxiety grew. She felt trapped as she scrolled through the classifieds. With every interview and every rejection letter that followed, Holly's worry loomed larger and stronger. Over time, Holly began to feel that it wasn't just the work she'd been doing that didn't matter;

she felt *she* no longer mattered. As a terrible depression took root, there was one thing that got her through those difficult days. It was the simple act of prayer.

A year before this crisis began, Holly had started attending a prayer group at her church. The group was exploring a wide range of different prayer traditions, including meditating, journaling, fasting, drawing, and dancing. What began as an intriguing intellectual exercise for Holly became her spiritual lifeline in that desperate time.

While walking through that dark valley of fear and anxiety, Holly became frustrated with the mask of self-assuredness she felt she needed to put on at the office and even with her closest friends. Yet when she began to open herself to God, she could voice her worries and frustrations. There was no one telling her to cheer up or suggesting that her situation wasn't really that bad. She wasn't forced to listen to a well-meaning family member telling her she was blowing things out of proportion. Instead, prayer gave her the space to feel the rejection and worry, in all their depth.

During the painful process, three things began to happen almost simultaneously. First, Holly began to feel peace. She was not sure exactly where it came from, but even through her tears and stomachaches, Holly felt an anchor of serenity that surpassed all of her understanding and stabilized her through her grief.

Second, Holly moved into a deeper sense of gratitude for everything she had. She noticed how the stream of thought that she whispered as she prayed would often turn into a flowing river of thankfulness. When she practiced walking meditation, she heard a rhythm setting the tempo for her list; each time she stepped she named something else that made her appreciative.

Finally, Holly began to sense God's steadfast love surrounding her. She realized that no matter what the organization thought of her job, even if all the hard work she'd done came down to a line item that could be easily blotted out of a budget, Holly knew that she was being held by her Creator, who delighted in her. Somehow, she began to understand that God loved her because of who she was and not because of what she accomplished.

Holly did walk through the dark valley and out to the other side. Though she would never want to go through the ordeal again, she learned a great deal in those six months. Mostly, she learned how the gift of prayer cultivates within us a sense of thankfulness for all we have, a deeper concern for the needs of others, and a core that allows us to rest in the steadfast love of God.

Developing Intuition

It is surely no coincidence that I really learned to trust my intuition shortly after my daughter was born. It was then that I learned intuition is a spiritual discipline, something one develops.[4] Intuition is a tool in the discernment process, which helps us become as wise as serpents. Intuition is the small voice we learn to identify, the internal wisdom that warns us and directs us. It is that fresh perspective that occurs to us when we are working out at the gym, the solution to a problem that comes to us when we are staring out into the water, the hidden thought that occurs to us while we are journaling, or the revelation of a dark truth that becomes unveiled as we walk and meditate.

There are people who equate intuition with God's voice. I am always hesitant to make that proclamation, because it is difficult to distinguish the voice of God from our own thoughts and dreams. There have been many times when I have felt compelled toward a particular path yet met a dead end. I have applied for numerous educational programs and jobs that I thought God was calling me to, and then I didn't get into the program or someone else got the position. I've known women who thought God wanted them to stay in abusive marriages. And we all know history is filled with gruesome stories of powerful men and women who thought they were doing something on behalf of the Divine, when everyone else could see their actions were really taken to benefit themselves, their political party, or their country. Just think of the Crusades or the current political power-mongering that occurs to the exclusion of feeding the hungry or providing medical care for the working poor. I realize that *it could happen to me. It could happen to anyone.*

It's far too easy for us to claim God's blessing on our own agendas. We can quickly replace the humility required to listen for God with a pride that assumes our thoughts are the same as God's. So, we listen for God with a bit of fear and trembling, a whole lot of humility, knowing we may not be right.

Of course, discerning God's voice in a safe environment, as part of a community that has learned to cultivate the art, can help guard against these abuses. If a person has a spiritual director or a gathering of two or three, then his or her conversations with God can be appreciated, welcomed, and assessed. When we are surrounded by a supportive community who is helping us discern and who feels free to agree or disagree with what we think we are hearing from God, then our listening for God can become a humbling experience rather than an exercise that places a divine rubber stamp on our own decisions.

I have begun to understand much of my time in prayer as being about developing my intuition. There is divine wisdom that can guide and direct us if we are able to stop and listen. Sometimes God is working through us and we do not realize it. Flashing images, catchy tunes, and seductive goods besiege us, but as the Hebrew language reminds us, God's Spirit is more like the wind, or a breath. God rarely yells at us as we speed along; instead, God invites us to stop and listen, with simple words like, "Be still and know that I am God."

Stillness is particularly difficult in this wired world that's filled with constant chatter. I imagine it was different for my grandmother, who spent many of her days working out in the fields chopping firewood or doing dishes in near silence. Throughout these methodic chores, there was room for her to breathe, to feel the wind, and to listen.

In contrast, when I was a teenager, I remember my father constantly yelling into my bedroom, "Will you turn that radio down? I can't hear myself think!" I would laugh with him as I turned down the volume, but soon after, I began carrying that radio in my pocket and listening on headphones. That way my father could think, and I learned to do things quite well with the background music. Now, I've realized that we often have to literally unplug to hear ourselves and to develop our intuition.

I certainly do not think my grandmother's day was any better than mine. I do not even think people were more spiritual back then. Yet I believe we will need to reframe the way we process information and the ways we listen for ourselves and for God. In our communities, we can embrace, encourage, and respect the fact that a person's intuition might lead her to take a path that does not seem to be the most logical or practical.

Our congregations need to be a place where a man with an Ivy League degree can announce that he wants to quit his job as a corporate executive and go into social work. They need to be the place where a woman can be supported for shining light on the white-collar crimes that her boss is committing. Our churches can embolden entrepreneurs to start new businesses. They can be communities where we take into account the stress of our bodies, the needs of our neighborhoods, and the passions of our lives—and places where we learn to trust the Holy Sprit who is moving and working through it all. Our churches need to provide a place where we stop and listen for that still, small voice whispering in every corner of our lives.

Rob learned the importance of intuition when he was facing a career change. He'd been unsatisfied with his job for some time, but could not say exactly why. When he began the process of developing his intuition, of listening for the still, small voice of God, he began to realize his un-fulfilled occupational expectations actually had a root in something else.

When his wife had left him several years earlier, Rob had been determined to "move on" quickly. He began putting more energy and effort into his job, while also pursuing a series of romantic relationships that didn't work out. His life was often in turmoil as he tried to extract love and a sense of security from climbing higher on the corporate ladder. As he began to develop his intuition, Rob realized his hunger would not be satiated with a new job. He began to work through the feelings of rejection that his wife's abandonment had stirred up and realized his misplaced affections. Throughout the following months, he began to listen for the Spirit and began to realize the security that comes from being loved by God.

By the end of this process, Rob no longer had the air of desperation and discontent that once followed him. He had finally stopped to listen for God. He had heard that still, small voice that whispered acceptance, and he stood as a man who knew he was a beloved child of God.

Seeking Direction

There was a time in our country when being born a girl meant you would likely grow up to become a schoolteacher or a secretary (at least until you got pregnant). But when I was growing up, I was told, over and over again, "You can be anything you want to be." This was good news for me, as it is for an entire generation of women. We are now hearing the same thing men were often told.

Cultural changes have also given men more freedom than they once had. It was once assumed a boy would grow up to take over the family business or step into the occupational role his father once inhabited. Now both men and women have more vocational choices, but that freedom brings with it other problems, like less career security in a shrinking job market. Young men and women often need to create their own jobs, small businesses, and even entire industries in order to survive in our current market.

It is that way not only with our occupations but also with so many things in our lives. While marriages were once arranged, or people used to marry within their own class, ethnicity, and religion, now we have much more freedom and choice in the matter. Beautiful unions are made across so many boundaries that were once taboo.

All this amazing choice, opportunity, and creativity can feel extremely liberating, but there is a downside to it as well. It is like when we stand in the grocery store in front of hundreds of hair-care products, staring at a myriad of promises and prices, and feel frozen in the face of the endless choices. We can also stand in the midst of our lives, paralyzed by the numerous options, wondering where we should go and what we should do. In these moments we must learn to seek guidance through prayer and spiritual direction. We learn to listen for God in the silence, through the Scriptures, and in the wisdom of one another.

Deborah Matthews, a pastor in Downers Grove, Illinois, was part of a group that helped her make difficult decisions. "There are a lot of ways we can make decisions about our lives," she recounted. "We can choose the path that is most lucrative, or the way that would be most exciting, but I wanted to think about my choices spiritually."

Deborah went through a process of discernment when she was trying to decide whether or not to pursue an additional master's degree while she was earning her Master's of Divinity. Meeting with a group that drew from the traditions of a Quaker clearness committee, Deborah brought a two-page written precis that focused on the decision she was trying to make and why it was so difficult. She explained to the group that even though she wanted a Master's Degree in Christian Spirituality, she was concerned about the extra money, energy, and time it would take to complete the additional education.

After presenting the written summary, Deborah talked about her feelings regarding the decision. Then the group sat in silence for five minutes, listening for God. After the time elapsed, one by one, people began to ask her questions like, "Which choice aligns you more with God's justice?" Or, "Which path directly relates to your future ministry?"

Deborah remembered one question in particular: "Which path brings more life?" As she started to articulate her answer, Deborah began to imagine a green, fertile jungle. The trees and vines that grew up in her mind were lush, beautiful, and shocking. She saw wild animals there and knew immediately that the path of more education would bring her more life.

The process did not stop there. Once Deborah made her decision, she continued to sense peace in it. Deborah worked hard and earned the additional degree, and has been thankful for the knowledge she gained. It has helped her be more centered in her ministry, allowed her to invite God into the most mundane church decisions, and shaped her understanding of the faith formation of every generation in the church. The path she chose has, indeed, brought her more life.

A college student in our congregation said it well as she reflected on what life was like after going through a major loss in her family. Looking toward her graduation in the midst of economic turmoil, she said, "I used to be totally career driven. All I would think about was what job I was going to get, and how I was going to climb the ladder for the next thirty years. Now, it's different. I'm thinking about my whole life. What will that look like? Loving and being loved by friends and family is crucial to me now. My profession is still important, but it's not everything." She had learned through her faith and practice to seek direction and to listen. As a result, she held a great wisdom even in the midst of turmoil.

Reordering Our Lives

When we take a more holistic approach to our spiritual lives, when we realize that God's presence surrounds us in our quotidian affairs, this helps us invite the Spirit to reorder our lives. This means acknowledging God's presence even in the corners of our lives that we sometimes keep hidden. For many of us, that deeply secret place has to do with our bank accounts.

While leading a workshop on stewardship, I asked people to tell a story from their childhoods about money. What did they learn about money when they were young? What sort of attitude did their parents have regarding money? How did they learn to spend or save? What sort of values did they have regarding money? What was their family's opinion of people who had more money than they had? Did they hide their money? Did they spend their money in a way that showed it off?

The most fascinating part of the discussion can be summed up in one response: "Money was something that was whispered about, late at night, when we children were supposed to be in bed. Mother would cry, and Father would say in a strained voice, 'I'm doing the best that I can.'"

Many of the stories echoed that one. The shocking thing was how money *wasn't* talked about. Money was a secret, a grown-up thing. Paying the bills was a source of great anxiety that no one could verbalize. As a pastor, I know this is still true. Often when an adult son or daughter tries to prepare a parent for elderly care, the biggest frustration can be the fact that the adult child does not know how much money the parent has. Even in our dependence, even when we need to rely completely on a family member, our cultural inclination to keep our financial situations secret remains.

I suppose this hiding worked for a long time for many middle-class Americans. Whenever we faced financial problems, we could quietly turn to our credit cards to solve them. Yet as many Americans have become more and more in debt, our shame has led us to talk even less about money. Hearing this stewardship workshop group reflect, realizing how uncomfortable we were discussing financial issues in our own homes, I understood why it is so difficult to talk about money in our churches. We carry all our worries, fears, frustrations, and shame with us as we sort out our congregational line items, our family's financial situations, and our personal budgets.

Most pastors hate to talk about stewardship of money, and parishioners resist it as well. Yet as our country faces more financial concerns, churches can no longer rely on their once-healthy endowments, and many generous givers have become more cautious. We are taking a

good, long look at our spending and saving habits, as individuals, institutions, churches, and a nation. Many churches struggle with basic
questions of whether they can keep their buildings or employ people.
Through this process, we realize the degree to which finances are a
spiritual force, and we are learning a new language around money.

In our church, meeting the financial crisis has been a long and
difficult process. Yet one of the most important things our elders did
was to spend some time in contemplative prayer before talking about
the budget. We were able to take that day, when men and women vie
for power, when we all have an agenda and a scheme, and invite God
into the midst of it.

We also need to seek God's direction as we talk about money within
our families. As men and women lose their jobs, as young adults and
retirees face massive economic pressures, we realize family life may have
to change. Indeed, many households already support intergenerational
family life, as roughly half the adults in their twenties cannot afford to
live on their own in the face of student loans, high rents, and stagnant
salaries. After college, in order to work their way out of their difficult
financial situation, many young men and women have moved back in
with their parents.

This economic shift encourages us to care for our families in ways
that run in contrast to cultural expectations. By listening to young
adults, we learn that lack of money does not always equate with a lack
of responsibility. While we used to mark adulthood by the ability of
a person to accumulate a wedding certificate and a mortgage, we've
found that many responsible adults need to move back in with their
parents. Many young men and women who went to college or bought
a home have not been able to avoid debt in the same way the generations before them did.

Within our families, we are realizing it may be healthier to rely on
one another rather than on high-interest credit cards to get us out of
emergency situations. People with parents whose retirement funds
shrank rapidly are beginning to reevaluate their living spaces, understanding that their homes will soon become an intergenerational refuge.

Some Christians are taking a thorough look at their finances, and
they are moving back to the practices of the early church as described
in Acts, where everyone shared as they each had need. New monastic
communities are forming as men as women live together in community,

often in urban, poverty-stricken areas, and imagining a new economy based on equal division of their resources and housework.

We are learning to verbalize our needs and expanding our ability to share. Communities are beginning to take the whispered conversations about the scarcity and abundance of money out of our bedrooms and talk about these issues in the light of day. Many prophets of our generation are beginning to rise up and call for radical redistribution, based on the message of Jesus.

In our personal lives, as we try to sort out our own attitudes about money, we are learning that we have put too much trust in our housing equity and our retirement funds. As they have lost value, many of us have an anxiety that goes beyond the numbers on our bank statement. In our churches, our families, and our personal lives, we are realizing that the economic turmoil is not just a financial issue but also a spiritual issue. We are learning that God's presence is a vital part of every part of our lives—even our bank accounts. We are recognizing our addiction to money and learning the prayer that we hear in the first steps of recovery meetings, "We admit that we are powerless over money—that our lives have become unmanageable. We came to believe that a Power greater than ourselves could restore us to sanity."

Communal Change

It may be a feeling of powerlessness amid the economic turmoil that has moved us to invite God into the most mundane aspects of our lives. Yet even before the calamity became apparent, we could sense the Holy Spirit moving in many congregations in vital ways. We are reaching back into our histories, learning from sacred practices of the past, and reframing those traditions in a new time and place. In the process, it seems that we are taking apart one other cultural dichotomy that has informed our religious life.

In the last few decades, an odd divide has crept into U.S. Christianity. Within the spectrum of Christian beliefs, there were two poles that understood the heart of the faith quit differently. On the one hand was the evangelical tradition, which emphasized the individual practices of prayer, devotion, and a personal relationship with Jesus Christ. Then, there was a more liberal tradition that focused on social justice, stressing the importance of alleviating poverty, hunger, and homelessness. The two extremes often seemed antithetical to each other.

Paul Raushenbush, the associate dean of religious life at Princeton University and religion editor of the *Huffington Post*, has personal experience with each of these two poles in Christianity. He was raised in a mainline denominational church, in a congregation that did a lot of social justice work but did not emphasize personal piety. Through addiction recovery, he learned to pray, and that became a path for him back to church. He found that these two streams within Christianity came together in his own life, giving strength to each other. Now, when Paul preaches in a progressive church, he makes it a point to tell the congregation that God loves them. "We need to hear that. In progressive churches, we often hear how God loves others, but it is important that we hear that God loves us."[5]

Right now, we are in the midst of a moment of change in our faithful history, as the two streams are flowing together more and more. Social-justice Christians are having a spiritual revival as they learn new ways to pray and discern. Or, maybe it's more accurate to say that we are reawakening to the strains within our own traditions that have always nurtured spirituality *and* social change. The spiritual writings of Howard Thurman and Dorothy Day are being rediscovered in a new time and place.

At the same time, an increased number of evangelicals are placing a priority on struggling for justice, feeding the hungry, and caring for creation. They are hearkening more to the people within their own tradition who have been working for these things all along, and yet have been a bit marginalized in the conversation in the last couple of decades.

In this new generation, as we struggle with our abuse of the earth, the inequities of our global economy, the crisis of our personal debt, and our national need for violence and destruction, our faithful communities are learning to overcome the dichotomies that once framed our religious dialogue. Instead, we are moving to a holistic approach to our faith, one that embraces the spiritual and the material, the sacred and the ordinary, piety and social justice. In the process, we invite God's direction into our decision making as we reorder every aspect of our lives.

Right now, our congregations are beginning to grapple with re-morse, as many of our national errors come to light. We know we will not be able to sustain unending growth in our financial markets at the same rate that we did in the last couple of decades. We will not be able to use coal, fossil fuels, and nuclear energy without any regard to what it is doing to our environment. We realize our predatory lending has led our nation into a cycle of shameful debt.

As a culture and as religious communities, we realize these are not just environmental and economic matters; they are also spiri-tual matters. We need to change our ways, not only because our past methods have been ineffective in reaching out in a new generation, but also because we have broken faith with the best of our traditions. Of course, change is difficult, both for individuals and organizations. But as Christian communities, repentance and transformation is the one discipline to which we are called on a regular basis.

Our Gospels begin with John the Baptist in the wilderness, with his wild clothes and diet, calling for us to repent, to change. And over our faithful history, our ability to open ourselves up and respond to the Spirit moving in new ways among us has caused us to be an extremely dynamic body. Now, we begin most of our services with a time of confession, asking God to change us. It is a good practice for us to be in, individually and as a community—to open ourselves up for radical transformation in every area of our lives.

Hope in the Desert

Hagar stood in the desert with her son Ishmael in her arms, the dust of the dry landscape swirling about her. She'd been the slave of Sarah, wife of Abraham, and her son was conceived when Hagar was forced to have a child with Abraham. But when Sarah finally and amazingly gave birth to her own son, Isaac, she urged Abraham to send Hagar and Ishmael away. The hostility drove Hagar and Ishmael out of their home and into the desert to die.

Abraham sent Hagar and Ishmael, the mother and his child, into the barren landscape with only a little bit of water. With no protection from the elements, Hagar walked in the hot sun until she and her child had consumed all of the water; they were parched, without a drop left.

As usual, the biblical story is scant, summing up a dramatic episode in a few short paragraphs. The ancient holy writers leave a lot to the imagination, and so I envision Hagar holding her child close, trying to soothe his dry, thirsty cries.

Finally, Hagar cannot bear to see his parched lips any longer, cannot stand that her words and desperate caresses no longer comfort him. So she places her son under a bush to die. As she walks away helplessly, trying to escape her child's cries, Hagar calls out to God, begging God to prevent her from seeing the death of her son.

At that moment of heart-wrenching distress, Hagar begins to understand she will be a mother of a great nation. It is as if she has somehow been given a taste of Abraham's covenant, when God promised Abraham his offspring would be as numerous as the grains of sand and the stars in the sky. It is after this realization that Hagar looks up and sees a well in the distance.

I wonder what stirred within Hagar that allowed her to imagine a great nation after having just relinquished her son? What caused her to look up from that barren ground and see living waters on the horizon? Was it the same sort of wondrous divinely inspired imagination that allowed Moses to lead men and women through miles of dusty landscape, driven by a vision of something completely different: a land flowing with milk and honey?

Our Scriptures are heavy with characters who became mothers of nations, saviors of people, and leaders of movements because they were somehow able to envisage that life-saving water as they stood in their particular desert. Even though every breath they took made their mouths as dry as dust, God gave them the imagination to hope.

Their examples have inspired a long history of people who have continued to dream of streams in the midst of barren deserts, rivers in dry wilderness, and milk flowing through inhospitable wastelands. In our day, we too can sense great hope in our own seemingly barren landscapes. What may have once been fertile land for our churches is now parched. Looking over our pews, many of us see the faithful remnant of a congregation from a half-century ago, and we wonder whether our churches will exist twenty years from now. In our denominations, churches that once boasted a membership of 3,000 have dwindled down to 150 members who can no longer afford to keep the church building running. Regularly, our governing bodies downsize and churches close.

Every once in a while, when we crack open our sanctuary doors and take a good look at what is outside, we hardly recognize the world in which we serve, because it has become so different from the one in which our churches were formed. Our denominational churches are no longer situated in the middle of a robust downtown, their proud steeples held erect through the hard work of dedicated housewives. We were seeing the world through a completely different frame then; we were working in a different context. And often those frames don't work in a new generation for a number of reasons.

Within our old frameworks, our church ministries reached out to a different family structure. We had churches that catered to nuclear families—ones with a mother, a father, and offspring. Our congregations often relied heavily on the volunteer work of housewives and geared programming and outreach to young families.

Now people get married and have children later in life, if at all. There is no longer a mom, a dad, and two-and-a-half children in each home. A good percentage of our households are likely to be single or in a same-gender relationship. The women of our congregations typically work at full-time jobs and have less free time to volunteer in the church.

Within our old frameworks, our churches could flourish in a Eurocentric society. Now, the ethnicity and culture of our nation has grown more diverse; we no longer live in the same context in which the particularly white Protestant church flourished. Since the Immigration Act of 1965, when national quotas were abolished and U.S. borders were opened to non-European immigrants, the rich diversity of the United States has become even more vibrant. Yet our mainline churches seldom reflect the diversity of the communities in which they are located.

Within our old frameworks, the people to whom our churches reached out were largely from a Christian background. Most of the people we welcomed into our congregations had been born and raised in the church. They could easily find their way around a Bible and could recite the Lord's Prayer and the Apostles' Creed on demand. These men and women knew those complicated hymns and were familiar with the flow and structure of the worship service.

Today, our neighborhoods are filled with people from a wide array of religious backgrounds and expressions. We struggle to communicate our faith in the midst of such pluralism and, in our worst expressions, we avoid or discriminate against those who are not Christians.

Within our old frameworks, we could rely on social conditioning and denominational loyalty to drive people to church. Now, we need to become much more intentional and caring as we reach out to our wider communities. Our modes of communication have changed so dramatically and so quickly that the church has struggled to keep up. The younger edge of our neighborhoods speaks fluently, instantly, globally, and interactively in the world of social media, while many of our congregations struggle to put together even a basic website.

Many of our denominational churches have found it difficult to thrive in the midst of these changes. Our message has been muted as we try to communicate from generation to generation. Sometimes, we've lost the vision to make our churches communities of welcome for our adult sons and daughters, the very people who could map out a course in our shifting deserts. They can easily communicate and minister to different family structures, an array of ethnicities, and among a variety of religious expressions.

The landscape has changed all around us. To some it feels like a desert—dry and barren, inhospitable, unable to sustain the next generation. Yet our common biblical story reminds us that we have a God who brings salvation to people who wander in the driest deserts. With a bit of divine imagination we will see the wells full of living water, as Hagar and Ishmael did. With a bit of divine imagination, we will see the milk and honey flowing all around us.

Even in the driest deserts we are beginning to see networks of tributaries flowing around us and vast constellations of stars sparkling above us. New opportunities, tools, movements, missions, and passions cascade through our wilderness landscape bringing vital ways of organizing faithful communities, communicating prayerful longings, and seeking social justice.

Organizing Faithful Communities

Streams are flowing in the desert as men and women begin to form spiritual community in response to the needs of our culture. Caleb is one of those people.

As a young adult, Caleb realized the autonomy he'd been taught to strive for was not working out the way he'd supposed it would. Caleb grew up in a working-class family from the Midwest. His father was a technician, and his mother was a housewife. Though they'd always struggled to pay the bills, Caleb spent his childhood in a nice home in a beautiful neighborhood, and he was constantly taught that the key to making it is working hard.

Caleb did work hard, starting with his first job at age fifteen. He was the first member of his family to go to college. But after receiving his degree, he'd been unable to find a job in his area of study. He ended up working at a grocery store, bagging food for minimum wage, without any insurance. He continued working hard, juggling various jobs and scraping by, until he developed a kidney stone. Since he lacked medical insurance, he kept putting off visiting a doctor, until one night when the pain forced him to go to the emergency room. To pay for that emergency room visit and the ongoing treatments, he maxed out his credit card, which left him in a cycle of debt that made it virtually impossible for Caleb to become financially secure again.

Sadly, even though Caleb's parents were doing fine financially, he never felt he could ask them for help. He'd been told too many times that independence was the most important thing he could develop, so he turned to the credit card he kept "for emergencies." Sitting in that hospital room, he realized the breakdown of society that allowed people to suffer with excruciating pain without access to medical care, the breakdown of our economic situation that allowed painfully high interest rates, and the breakdown of our families that made a person bear the weight of thousands of dollars of interest payments rather than borrow money from his own family. In short, he realized the folly of our culture of individualism, a culture with a threadbare safety net and predatory lenders happy to capitalize on others' needs.

Caleb understood that our distrust of institutions had led to a radical individualism that no longer works for our economy, our environment, our families, or ourselves. In response, he longed for something else. He longed for community. The time he'd spent in that emergency room, surrounded by people who needed so much, had a serious impact on how Caleb viewed life from that time forward. Caleb would no longer rely solely on himself. He realized that no amount of hard work could have kept him out of that situation.

Soon after that experience, Caleb went to seminary and now he is working to start a hospitality house in the tradition of Dorothy Day. It is a place that serves coffee and soup, a place that he hopes will grow into a center of community building and healing for his neighborhood. As he plans this spiritual community, Caleb understands that our ways of living and working together have changed in ways that particularly affect the church. Many people would rather gather with friends than spend a lot of energy propping up an institution. We seek out ways to come together in community; we want to form tribes. As I watch Caleb dream and work toward this new ministry, I cannot help but notice the vital spring of people surrounding him, supporting him. They are men and women who are looking toward the horizon, hoping for what might spring up.

Through Caleb's ministry, he longs to connect with those who are outside the religious mainstream. He is reaching out to the community by rethinking traditional pastoral boundaries, by allowing his weaknesses to be seen, and by loving the other, regardless.

In the past, many of our churches took pride in attracting the educated elite into our congregations. Yet, now that our landscape has changed, we must adjust and form communities that constantly push to the edges. We can imagine structures that have the wild freedom to allow new things to develop—ministries, churches, worship styles—and yet also have the order that allows for the rooting and grounding of tradition.

Communicating Prayerful Longings

Through the Internet and our ability to use it to publish theories, disseminate ideas, and organize people, community is forming and friendships are emerging. People who were once segregated are able to hear one another and live together in a different way.

Our communication has changed so we can easily move from face-to-face interactions to interfacing communications. Speaking to one another, seeing the expressions, and hearing the tremble in each voice has not waned in importance; it is just that we have additional tools that can enhance our personal narratives and make our interpersonal communication even deeper.

I was reminded of the depth and power of our stories and the way technology has shaped our sharing of them a few weeks ago when I got home from the office. As soon as I came in from the cold and set my laptop down, my husband asked with urgency, "Have you been following Twitter?"

"No. I had a meeting and needed to get some stuff done. Why?" I responded.

"Gideon committed suicide."

I looked at my husband with a blank stare, not quite believing it. Then, with nervous confusion, I began sorting through the mail in our living room and stacking the piles of paper into neater mounds until a wave of grief came over me.

I knew Gideon. I mean, I *sort of* knew Gideon. I never met him in real life, and yet I understood all sorts of things about him. We "talked" to each other often through regular updates on Twitter. Reading about the joys and struggles of Gideon's day became a part of my regular rhythm. He and I followed each other's updates for a long time before he realized I was the author of a book he'd had on his Amazon wishlist. Then when he read *Tribal Church*, we discussed the bits he highlighted.

I pored over his thoughtful prayers until they became my own. He was an intelligent young man, an Episcopalian, full of care and remorse, trying to sort out what he was going to do in the next step of his career. I remember one Twitter conversation in which I helped him prepare for a job interview. Like many young professionals, he was frustrated by a job market that had little room for new graduates. I knew his options were limited. But I never imagined that embracing death was a possibility he was considering.

When Gideon took his life, hundreds of people grieved. I heard the sorrow echoing from men and women across the country, from every sort of religious tradition. The despair rose, until it became clear how many people had prayed, complained, struggled, and studied with Gideon. As a compline of laments reverberated over the Twitter feed, it seemed that we were listening to a holy chorus. Living through the death of Gideon made me realize how this man's story, which had arisen through short updates and woven through so many lives, created a powerful community.

That evening, the Twitter status of Jon Fogle, a pastor in Pennsylvania, summed up our sentiments: "Anyone complaining about the superficiality of social networking wasn't paying attention today." Even in our grief, we found that constellation, giving us hope.

Seeking Social Justice

Looking at the landscape, we can see amazing life springing up on the edges of those rivers, especially when we as congregations begin to hear God's call to change the world. Activism has been a strong part of our lives together, and mainline denominations have been known for seeking justice in many areas of our country's history. Now, many congregations are focusing their attention on our stewardship of the environment.

One such community is First Presbyterian Church of Mount Airy, North Carolina. When the congregation began to plan for the church's 150th anniversary, they did many of the usual things as ways of celebrating their proud history. They created a historical room where they gathered old photos and other remembrances of the church's past. They invited a former minister back for the celebration. Yet, in that important moment, they decided that they did not just want to look back on the past, but they wanted to think about the future as well.

So, they began a series of green initiatives in order to advocate environmentalism inside and outside the church, like instituting a recycling program, replacing church lighting with CFL and LED lightbulbs, and educating the congregation on basic ways of "going green." Since it is a small town, their pastor, Steve Lindsley, reports that the local community is beginning to identify them as the "green church."

In a neighborhood where there is no curbside recycling, First Presbyterian may feel like a singular witness to our need to care for creation, but they are far from alone. One of the greatest concerns for the church in a new generation is that of the environment. We now understand that what we do to our portion of the earth right here affects the entire planet. We know we need to change our patterns of consumption.

As Christians in this particular moment, we understand our partnership with creation and the necessity for us to work in harmony, thankful for the gifts that God has given us. We are reminded not only that caring for creation was the first instruction given to us humans but also that such caring remains vital today.

Hope on the Horizon

Looking around at the shifts and changes, I have great hope for our churches. As we welcome the innovation and compassion of a new time, we realize that many of the longings of the current generation are the very things that we have been nurturing in our spiritual communities for hundreds of years.

When we look at our surroundings and ask ourselves where hope can be found, we see it in networks of living water flowing all around us. Communities of prayer and discernment are bubbling up with new life. As numerous as the stars in the sky, innovative men and women are using tools to reach out, to spread the good news, and to make a difference in the world. We are learning new ways to care for creation, and we realize that the church is often the central place to inform and educate.

In all this, God is giving us faith. In our work, we are taking the bits and pieces of people's shattered lives and opening ourselves up to God's work of creating caring, discerning communities—just as happened after a hurricane hit a small town in South Louisiana.

Walking around the area surveying the damage, it pained the pastor to see the houses torn apart and contents spilled on the ground in broken and tangled heaps. As he walked among the tree limbs, he saw in the dirt an image of a smiling face. Bending over to pick it up, he realized it was a wedding photo that the storm had ripped and discarded in the street.

Someone, somewhere, was missing the photo. He wondered who it could be. So, he decided to open the basement of his church and allow the community to have a photo lost and found. He set up long tables and invited the whole town to bring in any pictures they had picked up out of the storm debris.

People came with the bits of anonymous family histories: proud men standing in front of cherry-red Chevrolets, women posing in their Sunday best in front of bursting azalea bushes, anxious couples going to their high school dance, and small children playing on the park swings. Along with the crumpled bits of pictures, people began to pour into the fellowship hall, recognizing parts of their own lives and those of their neighbors.

Years after the fact, people still talk about the church that opened its doors to all the torn bits of people's lives. When I heard about it, I wondered what would happen if all our churches began to reach out to our communities, inviting people in so they might have some spiritual grounding in our cultural storm. Imagine: church as a space where men, women, and children can gather with the bits of their broken lives and seek wholeness with their stories, their histories, and their neighbors.

As I survey our metaphorical landscape, framing the possibilities, my mind turns back to Hagar, standing in that desert landscape with a scorched heart, suddenly full of courage. Can we, like Hagar, see great hope on the horizon? When we look at the shifting sands, when we see the stars glistening above, may we be reminded of what God can do.

Notes

Introduction: What Is the Substance of Our Hope?

1. In her article, "Does Ministry Fuel Addictive Behavior?" Sallie Morganthaler writes: "For over two decades, the entrepreneurial, multi-programmed church has been altering what people expect out of a church. The music they hear when they settle into their auditorium seats must compete with what's on their iPod. High-end visual technology during the worship service is, for many attendees, a given. In short, churchgoers expect a Sunday morning worship service to match their aesthetic experiences in the broader culture." Morganthaler explains how this high-pressure approach to ministry can be devastating for most pastors. *Church Leadership. Christianity Today Library.* January 1, 2006. http://www.ctlibrary.com/le/2006/winter/24.58.html.

2. Dave Kinnemann and Gabe Lyons, *UnChristian: What a New Generation Really Thinks about Christianity . . . and Why It Matters* (Grand Rapids: Baker Books, 2007), 25.

3. *Atlantic Monthly* has been tracking this demographic shift through the years. In his October 2006 article "Where the Brains Are," Richard Florida described "means migration" or "the mass relocation of highly skilled, highly educated, and highly paid Americans to a relatively small number of metropolitan regions," http://www.theatlantic.com/doc/200610/american-brains.

4. George Lakoff, *Whose Freedom? The Battle over America's Most Important Idea* (New York: MacMillan, 2006), 10–11.

5. Thomas Friedman, *Hot, Flat, and Crowded: Why We Need a Green Revolution—And How It Can Renew America* (New York: Farrar, Straus and Giroux, 2008), 5.

6. Phyllis Tickle, *The Great Emergence: How Christianity Is Changing and Why* (Grand Rapids: Baker Books, 2008), 15.

7. Barbara Brown Taylor, "Failing Christianity," *Christian Century,* June 2008, http://findarticles.com/p/articles/mi_m1058/is_12_125/ai_n27497060?tag=content;col1.

8. Diana Butler Bass, *A People's History of Christianity* (San Francisco: Harper-One, 2009). Bass's book provides a beautiful resource for those who are interested in the historic streams of thought that led to so many of our present spiritual movements.

9. Kibbie Simmons Ruth, Karen McClintock, *Healthy Disclosures* (Herndon, VA: Alban Institute, 2007).

10. Christopher Hitchens, *God Is Not Great: How Religion Poisons Everything* (New York: Twelve, Hatchett Book Group, 2007).

11. Matt Dellinger, "Road Worriers," *Atlantic Monthly,* January/February 2009, http://www.theatlantic.com/doc/200901/new-urbanists.

12. Diana Butler Bass, *Christianity for the Rest of Us: How the Neighborhood Church Is Transforming the Faith* (San Francisco: HarperOne, 2007), 41–42.

13. Eric Greenberg and Karl Weber, *Generation We: How Millennial Youth Are Taking Over America and Changing Our World Forever* (Emeryville, CA: Pachatusan, 2008).

14. Neil Howe and William Strauss, "The Next 20 Years: How Customer and Workforce Attitudes Will Evolve," *Harvard Business Review,* July-August 2007.

Chapter 1: Redistributing Authority

1. Pew Forum on Religion and Public Life, "U.S. Religious Landscape Survey: Religious Affiliation: Diverse and Dynamic" (Washington: Pew Research Center, 2008), http://religions.pewforum.org/pdf/report-religious-landscape-study-full.pdf.

2. Lawrence Lessig, *Free Culture: How Big Media Uses Technology and the Law to Lock Down Culture and Control Creativity* (New York: Penguin Group, 2004), 27–28.

3. Tony Jones writes about the emerging church in *The New Christians* (San Francisco: Jossey-Bass, 2008). Two examples of "loyal radicals" who pastor in innovative ways while remaining committed to their denominations are Nadia Bolz-Weber, founding pastor of House for All Sinners and Saints and author of *Salvation on the Small Screen? Twenty-four Hours of Christian Television* (New York: Seabury Books, 2008), and Nannette Sawyer, founding pastor of Wicker Park Grace and author of *Hospitality the Sacred Art: Discovering the Hidden Spiritual Power of Invitation and Welcome* (Woodstock, VT: Skylight Paths Publishing, 2007). Jonathan Wilson-Hartgove wrote *New Monasticism: What It Has to Say to Today's Church* (Grand Rapids: Brazos Press, 2008).

4. *Modernism: Designing a New World 1914–1939* (Washington: Corcoran Gallery of Art, 2008), http://www.corcoran.org/Modernism/index.htm.

5. Thomas Friedman, *Hot, Flat, and Crowded: Why We Need a Green Revolution—And How It Can Renew America* (New York: Farrar, Straus and Giroux, 2008), 43.

6. Bill McKibben, *Deep Economy: The Wealth of Communities and the Durable Future* (New York: Holt Paperbacks, 2007), 5–11.

7. Michael Pollan, *The Omnivore's Dilemma: A Natural History of Four Meals* (New York: The Penguin Press, 2006), 110–111.

8. McKibben, *Deep Economy*, 107. McKibben points out that "counties with Wal-Marts have grown poorer than surrounding counties, and the more Wal-Marts they had, the faster they grew poorer."

9. David Williams, pastor of Trinity Presbyterian Church in Bethesda, often writes of the transition of the church from the big steeple to the big parking lot. He blogs at BelovedSpear.org.

10. Kinnemann and Lyons, *UnChristian*, 67.

11. Sally Morgenthaler, "Does Ministry Fuel Addictive Behavior?" ChristianityTodayLibrary.com. http://www.ctlibrary.com/le/2006/winter/24.58.html.

12 McKibben, *Deep Economy*, 34–36.

13. Chris Anderson, *The Long Tail: Why the Future of Business Is Selling Less of More.* (New York: Hyperion Books, 2008), 8–9. Anderson, the editor-in-chief of *Wired* magazine, largely follows music as he explains that we have moved from a culture of hits to one of hits and niches. The Internet makes consumers less dependent on the physical inventory on a small store and allows lesser known authors, musicians, and artists to sell more. Of course, in this movement, we see conglomeration and dissemination working at the same time, because companies that are learning to sell niche products are getting bigger and bigger. Amazon is one example.

14. In *Tribal Church: Ministering to the Missing Generation* (Herndon, VA: Alban Institute, 2007), I write about the need for economic understanding while ministering to young adults. The economic frustrations that were hidden when that book was published have come to light more in recent years.

15. Diana Butler Bass, *Christianity for the Rest of Us*, 41–42. Bass talks at great length about the "new village church."

16. Deloitte Touche Tohmatsu, "The State of the Media Democracy: Are You Ready for the Future of Media?" 2007, http://images.digitalmedianet.com/2007/Week_30/uj1ex4vc/story/deloittemediademocracysurvey.pdf. The survey states that television viewing is down for younger generations, while the creation of and demand for user-generated content is up.

17. Nadia Bolz-Weber, Carol Howard Merritt, and Bruce Reyes-Chow, "Bruce and Carol Talk with Nadia Bolz-Weber," *God Complex Radio*, June 1, 2009, http://www.blogtalkradio.com/godcomplexradio/2009/06/01/Bruce-and-Carol-Talk-with-Nadia-Bolz-Weber.

18. Edward Cody, "Deadly Crackdown Intensifies in Burma," *The Washington Post*, September 28, 2007.

Chapter 2: Re-forming Community

1. Thom S. Rainer, *The Bridger Generation* (Nashville: Broadman and Holman Publishers, 2006), 3–5.

2. To this day, the Builders in our congregations are often the church members most concerned about painting the doors, repairing the boilers, and making sure that the roof is maintained.

3. David Brooks, *Bobos in Paradise: The New Upper Class and How They Got There* (New York: Simon & Schuster, 2000), 21–22.

4. Brooks, 25–30.

5. Neil Howe and William Strauss, "The Next 20 Years: How Customer and Workforce Attitudes Will Evolve," *Harvard Business Review,* July-August 2007. Though the age of Generation X is fluid, I typically look to Strauss and Howe's research for defining the dates.

6. McKibben, *Deep Economy,* 112–114.

7. Eric Gorski, "Dobson resigns as Chairman of Focus on the Family," *The San Francisco Chronicle,* February 27, 2009. The AP article points out that young evangelicals are discontent with FOF's narrow focus on abortion and gay marriage.

8. Christine Wicker, *The Fall of the Evangelical Nation: The Surprising Crisis inside the Church* (San Francisco: HarperOne, 2007).

9. Howe and Strauss, "The Next 20 Years," 45.

10. Phyllis Tickle, *The Great Emergence: How Christianity Is Changing and Why* (Grand Rapids: Baker Books), 2008. Presbymergents use the term "Loyal Radicals" to describe themselves. Adam Walker Cleaveland, who cofounded Presbymergents with Karen Sloan, siad that he first heard the term from Bob Hopkins, who is a Mission Shaped Ministry Developer and coach for Fresh Expressions in the United Kingdom.

11. Tony Jones, *The New Christians: Dispatches from the Emergent Frontier* (San Francisco: Jossey Bass), 41–43

12. Jones, *New Christians,* 9–10.

13. Therein lies a conundrum of innovative pastoral leadership: congregations often thrive with good leadership, but if there is no solid structure, members tend to become tied to the pastor rather than to each other.

14. Of course, new churches are not the only one struggling with finances. Our traditional church model is breaking down as well. In the Presbyterian church, about 40 percent of our congregations do not have a large enough membership to support a full-time pastor.

15. Diana Butler Bass expands on "fluid retraditioning" in *The Practicing Congregation: Imagining a New Old Church* (Herndon, VA: The Alban Institute, 2004), 42.

Chapter 3: Reexamining the Medium

1. Some details of this story have been changed to protect the identity of the parishioner.

2. Seth Godin, *Tribes: We Need You to Lead Us* (New York: Penguin Group, 2008), 3–5.

3. Marshall McLuhan, *Understanding Media: The Extensions of Man* (Cambridge: The MIT Press, 1994). McLuhan's laws of media were visionary and McLuhan inspired and foresaw many technological innovations. His laws include the law of extension, that every technology amplifies or extends some organ or faculty of the user. Now, we can see how social media amplifies or enhances aspects of social culture.

4. Allison Fine, *Momentum: Igniting Social Change in a Connected Age* (San Francisco: Jossey-Bass, 2006).

5. Tickle, *The Great Emergence,* 151–153.

6. David Kenny and John F. Marshall, "Contextual Marketing: The Real Business of the Internet," *Harvard Business Review on Marketing* (Boston: Harvard Business School Press, 1999), 69–85. Though this chapter was written more than ten years ago, Kenny and Marshall correctly forecast the transition from a destination website to the ubiquitous Internet.

7. The Moderator of the Presbyterian Church (USA) is the highest elected official of the denomination.

8. Daniel Solove, *The Future of Reputation: Gossip, Rumor, and Privacy on the Internet* (New Haven: Yale University Press, 2007), 12.

9. Mike Yaconelli, *Messy Spirituality* (Grand Rapids: Zondervan, 2002).

10. Solove, *Reputation,* 9.

11. Many people don't realize that people in the same city or area may have access to your Facebook site. Of course, there are many privacy settings that people can use to make sure that your reputation is not being jeopardized on Facebook.

12. Phillip Zimbardo, *The Lucifer Effect: Understanding How Good People Turn Evil* (New York: Random House, 2007), 289–307.

13. Zimbardo, *Lucifer,* 367–368.

14. Malcolm Gladwell, *Blink: The Power of Thinking without Thinking* (New York: Little, Brown and Company, 2005), 239.

15. Emmanuel Levinas, *The Levinas Reader* (Malden, MA: Blackwell Publishers, Inc, 1989), 75.

Chapter 4: Retelling the Message

1. Jean M. Twenge, *Generation Me: Why Today's Young Americans Are More Confident, Assertive, Entitled—And More Miserable Than Ever Before* (New York:

Free Press, 2006), 169. Twenge sees social media as evidence of young Americans' narcissism.

2. Daniel H. Pink, *A Whole New Mind: Why Right-Brainers Will Rule the Future* (New York: Riverhead Books, 2005), 100–101.

3. Pink, *New Mind*, 103.

4. Carl Jung, *The Portable Jung* (New York: Penguin, 1976), 59–60.

5. Karen Armstrong, *The Case for God* (New York: Alfred A. Knopf, 2009), ix. Armstrong talks about the different ways ancient Greeks had for collecting knowledge. They understood things in terms of *logos* and *mythos*. While *logos* referred to scientific understandings, *mythos* pertained to the mysteries of life. In our modern age, we began to confuse the two.

6. These thoughts formed with the insights of my colleagues Ashley Goff and Tara Spuhler McCabe.

7. McKibben, *Deep Economy*, 111. McKibben writes that "the incidence of depression exploded in the twentieth century" and he writes that it is not just a matter of labeling. Even when researchers use nonmedical terms, the rise in depression is startling.

8. Godin, *Tribes*. Godin has a very interesting discussion on faith, religion, and tribes, 82–84.

Chapter 5: Reinventing Activism

1. As I write, I am having a Twitter conversation about the reign of God, so my words also reflect some of the opinions of Nanette Sawyer, Andrew Tatusko, Landon Whitsitt, and Fritz Gutwein.

2. This story was originally published on Adam Walker Cleaveland's blog *Pomomusings*, at http://pomomusings.com/2008/02/04/carol-howard-merritt-on-the-kingdom-of-god/ as a part of his guest blogger series on the kingdom of God.

3. Paul Raushenbush, ed. *Christianity and the Social Crisis in the 21st Century* (San Francisco: HarperOne, 2007).

4. Shane Claiborne, *The Irresistible Revolution: Living as an Ordinary Radical* (Grand Rapids: Zondervan, 2006). Brian McLaren, *Everything Must Change: Jesus, Global Crises, and a Revolution of Hope* (Nashville: Thomas Nelson, 2007). Eric Elnes, *The Phoenix Affirmations: A New Vision for the Future of Christianity* (San Francisco: Jossey-Bass, 2006). Sara Miles, *Take This Bread: A Radical Conversion* (New York: Ballantine Books, 2007). Julie Clawson, *Everyday Justice: The Global Impact of Our Daily Choices* (Grand Rapids: Zondervan, 2009).

5. For two interesting perspectives, see Martha Honey, *Ecotourism and Sustainable Development: Who Owns Paradise?* (Washington: Island Press, 1998) and Don Richter, *Mission Trips that Matter* (Nashville: Upper Room Press, 2008).

6. Joseph E. Stiglitz, *Globalization and Its Discontents* (New York: Norton, 2002), 4. Stiglitz explains how globalization has reduced the sense of isolation that many people in the developing world felt, and he describes how links that are forged through the Internet have brought about important protests and change, like the international landmines treaty.

7. Cory Doctorow, "For Love of Water: Infuriating and Incredible Documentary about the World Water Crisis," http://boingboing.net/2008/04/07/for-love-of-water-in.html.

8. Michel Foucault wrote extensively about the relationship between knowledge and power, and the relationship has become understood. See, for instance, *Power/Knowledge: Selected Interviews & Other Writings, 1972–1977* (New York: Pantheon Books, 1980). I would add that as we gain knowledge we have a greater burden of responsibility.

9. David Batstone, *Not for Sale: The Return of the Global Slave Trade* (San Francisco: HarperOne, 2007). I interview David Batstone on our *God Complex Radio* podcast. http://godcomplexradio.com/2010/02/season-1-episode-6-david-batstone-not-for-sale/

Chapter 6: Renewing Creation

1. Jack Hitts, *This American Life*, "110: Mapping," http://www.thisamericanlife. org/Radio_Episode.aspx?sched=921. Jack Hitts visits Toby Lester, who maps all of the buzzing sounds that surround him. The episode made me aware of all the humming that goes on around us.

2. Richard Louv, *Last Child in the Woods: Saving Our Children from Nature-Deficit Disorder* (Chapel Hill, NC: Algonquin Books of Chapel Hill, 2005), 115–117.

3. Stuart B. Levy, "Antibacterial Household Products: Cause for Concern," Centers for Disease Control and Prevention website, http://www.cdc.gov/ncidod/eid/vol7no3_supp/levy.htm.

4. Thomas Friedman, *Hot, Flat, and Crowded: Why We Need a Green Revolution—And How It Can Renew America* (New York: Farrar, Straus and Giroux, 2008), 31–33.

5. Many prominent evangelical leaders signed an open letter prior to the 2004 elections, which stated: "God put human beings on the earth to 'subdue it' and to 'have dominion' over the animals (Gen. 1:28) . . . The Bible does not view 'untouched nature' as the ideal state of the earth, but expects human beings to develop and use the earth's resources wisely for mankind's needs (Gen. 1:28; 2:15; 9:3; 1 Tim. 4:4). In fact, we believe that public policy based on the idealism of 'untouched nature' hinders wise development of the earth's resources and thus contributes to famine, starvation, disease, and death among the poor. We believe the ethical choice is for candidates who will allow resources to be developed and

used wisely, not for candidates indebted to environmental theories that oppose nearly all economic development in our nation and around the world," http://www. epm.org/resources/2010/Mar/2/biblical-and-ethical-issues-have-bearing-election/.

6. Greenberg and Weber, *Generation We*, 43.

7. John Fife, a retired Presbyterian pastor and former moderator of the General Assembly, reminded me of this during his sermon on August 3, 2009, at the Montreat Youth Conference.

8. Christopher Hitchens, *God Is Not Great: How Religion Poisons Everything* (New York: Twelve Books, 2007). 46–47. Hitchens, an atheist, says the attitude of religion toward science is often necessarily hostile, "A modern believer can say and even believe that his [sic] faith is quite compatible with science and medicine, but the awkward fact will always be that both things often have a tendency to break religion's monopoly, and have often been fiercely resisted for that reason."

9. Diana Butler Bass, *People's History of Christianity*, 36–38.

10. Linda O. McMurry, *George Washington Carver: Scientist and Symbol* (Oxford: Oxford University Press, 1981), 219.

11. Louv, *Last Child*, 291.

12. Louv, *Last Child*, 99–112.

13. Rob Stein, "Millions of Children in U.S. Found to Be Lacking Vitamin D," *Washington Post*, August 3, 2009.

14. The curriculum was written in large part by Susan Fellows.

15. For more on the Water Bottle Pledge, see the *Presbyterians for Earth Care* site, http://www.presbyearthcare.org/advocacy-h20.html.

16. Charles Duhigg, "Clean Water Laws Are Neglected, at a Cost in Suffering," *New York Times*, September 12, 2009.

Chapter 7: Retraditioning Spirituality

1. Brian McLaren questions many of the dichotomies and labels that we use in his book, *A Generous Orthodoxy: Why I Am a Missional, Evangelical, Post/Protestant, Liberal/Conservative, Mystical/Poetic, Biblical, Charismatic/Contemplative, Fundamentalist/Calvinist, Anabaptist/Anglican, Methodist, Catholic, Green, Incarnational, Depressed-yet-Hopeful, Emergent, Unfinished CHRISTIAN* (El Cajon, CA: Youth Specialties, 2004).

2. The yearning for physical touch can manifest itself in very odd ways sometimes. While in the 1960s people may have participated in "Love Ins," in the last several years "Cuddle Parties" became a trend. In these gatherings, non-sexual touch, spooning, and snuggling are encouraged among strangers.

3. Not everyone agrees with me on this point. For instance, my friends Neal Locke and Kimberly Knight, who pastor virtual churches in Second Life, seem to

have a deeper sense of virtual community than I have. Neal, in particular, speaks of flesh-and-blood presence as "meat space" and often argues that online presence is *more* meaningful.

4. Carl Jung writes about intuition, and the Myers-Briggs personality assessment has popularized the idea. Often, I find that Jung's ideas of synchronicity and intuition are a way for people to become open to the ways in which God is working in their lives. For more on this subject, see Carl Jung, *The Portable Jung* (New York: Penguin Books, 1971), 178–272, 505–518.

5. Paul Raushenbush, phone interview with author, May 14, 2009.